Betty Crocker's

RED SPOON COLLECTION™

BEST RECIPES FOR SOUPS AND SANDWICHES

PRENTICE HALL PRESS

New York   London   Toronto   Sydney   Tokyo   Singapore

PRENTICE HALL PRESS
15 Columbus Circle
New York, New York 10023

Published simultaneously in Canada by Prentice Hall Canada Inc.

Library of Congress Cataloging-in-Publication Data

Best recipes for soups and sandwiches.
    p.   cm.—(Betty Crocker's red spoon collection)
  Includes index.
ISBN 0-13-068347-7
  1. Soups   2. Sandwiches   I. Series.
TX757.B42   1991
641.8′13—dc20   90-39878
                                                              CIP

Manufactured in the United States of America

        10   9   8   7   6   5   4   3   2   1

              First Edition

*Front Cover: Turkey and Avocado
Club Sandwiches (page 75) and
Gazpacho (page 25)*

CONTENTS

INTRODUCTION

Soups and sandwiches go together like peanut butter and jelly, meat and potatoes or any other favorite food pairings. Soups and sandwiches are always popular because of their easy preparation and comfortable, informal serving possibilities. We all have our favorite sandwich: a classic grilled cheese, an overstuffed Dagwood or a crunchy taco. In midwinter there is nothing quite as satisfying as a steaming hot bowl of thick, hearty chowder, and in the heat of summer, there is nothing like a cool, creamy potato soup. However you pair them, soups and sandwiches are always satisfying.

We've provided a wide variety of soups and sandwiches in this book, from tried-and-true favorites to international adventures—mix them and match them for exciting meals. We've also paired soups and sandwiches in the color photographs, to provide added inspiration and interesting suggestions for meal planning. Soups and sandwiches allow busy cooks to relax, be flexible and improvise.

The sandwich is the original "convenience" food. Legend has it that John Montagu, the fourth earl of Sandwich, who lived in the mid-nineteenth century, was too attached to the gaming table to tear himself away for dinner. Instead, when hunger struck he ordered meat between two slices of bread to be brought and set down right next to his stack of chips, so that he could eat without interrupting his gaming.

Montagu's invention was born of ingenuity, and your sandwiches can be just as inventive and creative. Don't be afraid to try new combinations, fillings and spreads. Imagine the first person who dared to combine bacon, lettuce and tomato! You may well find a combination as fresh and delicious. In these pages you'll find many sandwiches to pique your curiosity as well as your appetite. You'll want to sample them at lunch, for dinner on the run or when entertaining.

We often think of sandwiches as quick, casual meals, but they can also be much more. Of course they're the perfect middle-of-the-night feast, and they're the most popular lunch in town—or country. But sandwiches can be wonderfully elegant and sophisticated. Try Watercress Triangles (page 57), a Shrimp and Avocado Club Sandwich (page 75) or Caviar Canapés (page 60). Your preconceptions will disappear almost as quickly as these sandwiches do at a cocktail party!

We've gathered our most popular and satisfying hearty sandwiches here as well.

They range from simple Hoagie Sandwiches (page 67) to the extravagant Muffuletta (page 69). Hot or cold, on pita, croissants or rolls, as appetizers or main dishes, they're all here—and sure to please. Sandwiches are loved by everyone, from the smallest child to the most sophisticated adult. For casual get-togethers and even for family dinners, you can set up a buffet of sandwich fixings. Then everyone can make their own favorites, or create new combinations.

You can turn to the Red Spoon Tips (pages 97–108) at the back of this book for information on how to prepare sandwiches ahead of time, recipes for flavored butters and mayonnaises and menus for many occasions. We've even included a bread recipe because there's nothing quite like a sandwich made on crusty, fresh-from-the-oven bread.

Of course, that bread will taste just as delicious dunked in a bowl of hot, hearty soup. After skating, skiing, taking a brisk walk or even after a long, hard day relaxing on the sofa and reading a book, a bubbling pot of soup or stew, filling your kitchen with the aromas of smoky ham, onion and herbs, is the perfect prelude to a satisfying dinner.

Soup is incredibly versatile; it can begin a full meal, or it can be a meal within itself. Try Cold Potato Soup (page 23) as an elegant starter for a meal, served either hot or cold. Or set out big bowls of soup with lots of fresh bread for dipping, and you have an easy, complete meal—perfect for fixing ahead of time.

Soups can be as simple as a clear broth (see the recipes for four basic broths in the Red Spoon Tips), or as hearty as Smoky Bean Soup (page 28). You can make a Black Bean Soup (page 28) that will rival your grandmother's or you can whip up a quick batch of Easy Spinach Soup (page 18) to complement a grilled cheese sandwich for Saturday's lunch.

Try a cold soup like Gazpacho (page 25), cucumber or vegetable—it's wonderfully refreshing on a hot summer's day. And don't forget to try the fruit soups. You'll love their fresh taste, perfect when topped with a dollop of sour cream.

Soup is satisfying at home, but it's also perfect for lunch at the office or at school. You can make soup over the weekend and enjoy it for lunch during the week.

Although stirring a long-simmering soup is fun and soul-satisfying, we know that sometimes you just can't spend the time to make a soup from scratch. We've included many recipes that don't take very long and that use prepared ingredients, such as canned soup and instant bouillon that you probably already have on hand. You'll also find instructions for using bouillon as a shortcut in your homemade soup in the Red Spoon Tips.

Soups and sandwiches are fabulous either individually or together. We're sure that you'll find these recipes easy to make and always delicious. And if you're looking for new menu ideas, try some of the menus in the Red Spoon Tips. Remember, soups and sandwiches are generally easy to vary, so experiment with different flavors and combinations. You never know what you'll come up with—it may be as wonderful as the BLT turned out to be. Enjoy these recipes—whether for family, friends or midnight snacks.

· 1 ·
LIGHT SOUPS

Clear Japanese Soup

3 cups chicken broth
1 teaspoon soy sauce
Garnishes (thinly sliced mushrooms, green
   onion strips, celery leaves, thinly
   sliced lemon or lime, thinly sliced
   carrot, strips of lemon peel)

Heat broth and soy sauce to boiling, stirring occasionally. Top each serving with 1 to 3 garnishes.

Egg Drop Soup

3 cups chicken broth
1 teaspoon salt
Dash of white pepper
1 medium green onion chopped
   (with top)
2 eggs, slightly beaten

Heat chicken broth, salt and white pepper to boiling in 2-quart saucepan. Stir green onion into eggs. Pour egg mixture slowly into broth, stirring constantly with fork, to form shreds of egg.

Following pages: Clear Japanese Soup and Caviar Canapés (page 60)

Chicken-Vegetable Soup

3 cups eight-vegetable juice
2 cups water
5 cups finely chopped cabbage
1 medium onion, sliced
4 medium carrots, cut into 1/4-inch slices
    (about 2 cups)
2 medium stalks celery, chopped (about
    1 cup)
2 tablespoons instant chicken bouillon
1/4 teaspoon pepper
3-pound broiler-fryer chicken, cut up and
    skinned
1/2 teaspoon salt
1/2 teaspoon paprika
2 tablespoons margarine or butter

Heat eight-vegetable juice, water, cabbage, onion, carrots, celery, bouillon (dry) and pepper to boiling in 4-quart Dutch oven; reduce heat. Cover and simmer 30 minutes.

Remove excess fat from chicken; cut each chicken breast half into halves; sprinkle chicken with salt and paprika. Heat margarine in 10-inch skillet over medium heat until hot. Cook chicken in margarine until light brown on all sides, 15 to 20 minutes. Add chicken to soup. Heat to boiling; reduce heat.

Cover and simmer until chicken is done, about 30 minutes longer. Place chicken in soup bowls; pour soup over chicken.

Chicken Soup with Leeks

3-pound broiler-fryer chicken, cut up and
    skinned
4 cups water
1/2 cup uncooked barley
1 medium carrot, sliced (about 1/2 cup)
1 medium stalk celery, sliced (about
    1/2 cup)
2 teaspoons salt
2 teaspoons instant chicken bouillon
1/4 teaspoon pepper
1 bay leaf
1 1/2 cups sliced leeks (with tops)

Remove excess fat from chicken. Heat all ingredients except leeks to boiling in 4-quart Dutch oven; reduce heat. Cover and simmer 30 minutes.

Stir in leeks. Heat to boiling; reduce heat. Cover and simmer until thickest pieces of chicken are done, about 15 minutes. Remove chicken; cool slightly. Remove meat from bones; cut into 1-inch pieces. Skim fat from broth; remove bay leaf. Add chicken to broth; heat until hot, about 5 minutes.

Chicken-Noodle Soup with Vegetables

2¹/₂- to 3-pound broiler-fryer chicken,
    cut up
4 cups water
1¹/₂ teaspoons salt
1 teaspoon sugar
¹/₄ teaspoon pepper
3 chicken bouillon cubes or 3 teaspoons
    instant chicken bouillon
4 medium carrots, cut into ¹/₂-inch slices
    (about 2 cups)
4 medium stalks celery, cut into ¹/₂-inch
    slices (about 2 cups)
2 cups uncooked thin egg noodles

Remove any excess fat from chicken. Place chicken, giblets (except liver) and neck in Dutch oven. Add remaining ingredients except noodles. Heat to boiling; reduce heat. Cover and simmer until thickest pieces of chicken are done, about 45 minutes.

Cook noodles as directed on package. Remove chicken from broth; cool chicken 10 minutes. Skim fat from broth; strain broth. Remove chicken from bones and skin; cut chicken into bite-size pieces. Add chicken and noodles to broth; heat until hot, about 5 minutes.

Mulligatawny Soup

2¹/₂- to 3-pound broiler-fryer chicken,
    cut up
4 cups water
1¹/₂ teaspoons salt
1 teaspoon curry powder
1 teaspoon lemon juice
¹/₈ teaspoon ground cloves
¹/₈ teaspoon ground mace
1 medium onion, chopped (about ¹/₂ cup)
2 tablespoons margarine or butter
2 tablespoons all-purpose flour
2 tomatoes, chopped
1 medium carrot, thinly sliced (about
    ¹/₂ cup)
1 apple, chopped
1 green pepper, cut into ¹/₂-inch pieces
Snipped parsley

Remove any excess fat from chicken. Heat chicken, giblets (except liver), neck, water, salt, curry powder, lemon juice, cloves and mace to boiling in Dutch oven; reduce heat. Cover and simmer until thickest pieces of chicken are done, about 45 minutes.

Remove chicken from broth; cool chicken 10 minutes. Remove chicken from bones and skin; cut chicken into bite-size pieces. Skim fat from broth; strain broth. Add enough water to broth, if necessary, to measure 4 cups.

Cook and stir onion in margarine in Dutch oven until tender. Remove from heat; stir in flour. Gradually stir in broth. Add chicken, tomatoes, carrot, apple and green pepper. Heat to boiling; reduce heat. Cover and simmer until carrot is tender, about 10 minutes. Garnish each serving with parsley.

Turkey-Rice Soup

1 turkey carcass
8 cups water
2½ teaspoons salt
¼ teaspoon pepper
1 bay leaf
½ cup uncooked brown or regular rice
2 medium stalks celery, chopped (about
    1 cup)
1 medium onion, chopped (about ½ cup)
1 carrot, cut into 1-inch pieces
1 can (16 ounces) whole tomatoes,
    undrained

Break up turkey carcass to fit 8-quart Dutch oven. Add water, salt, pepper and bay leaf. Heat to boiling; reduce heat. Cover and simmer 1½ hours.

Remove bones from broth; cool 10 minutes. Remove turkey from bones; cut turkey into bite-size pieces. Strain broth. Add turkey, rice, celery, onion and carrot to broth in Dutch oven. Heat to boiling; reduce heat. Cover and simmer until rice is tender, about 30 minutes. Stir in tomatoes; break up with fork. Heat until hot. Remove bay leaf; serve.

Fish and Vegetable Soup

1 small cucumber
5 cups chicken broth
1 tablespoon soy sauce
⅛ teaspoon ground ginger
Dash of pepper
2 ounces uncooked vermicelli
½ pound fish fillets, cut into ½-inch slices
1 can (4¼ ounces) tiny shrimp, rinsed
    and drained
1 cup sliced mushrooms or 1 can
    (4 ounces) mushroom stems and pieces,
    drained
5 cups torn spinach (about 4 ounces)
¼ cup sliced green onions (with tops)

Cut cucumber lengthwise into halves; remove seeds. Cut each half crosswise into thin slices. Heat chicken broth, soy sauce, ginger and pepper to boiling in 3-quart saucepan; stir in vermicelli. Heat to boiling; cook uncovered just until tender, about 4 minutes. Stir in cucumber, fish, shrimp and mushrooms. Heat to boiling; reduce heat. Simmer uncovered until fish flakes easily with fork, about 1 minute. Stir in spinach until wilted. Sprinkle each serving with green onions.

Fish and Lettuce Soup

½ pound walleye fillets
1 teaspoon cornstarch
2 teaspoons vegetable oil
½ teaspoon salt
½ teaspoon soy sauce
¼ teaspoon sesame oil
Dash of white pepper
½ head iceberg lettuce
4 cups chicken broth
1 teaspoon salt
1 green onion (with top), chopped

Cut fish crosswise into ½-inch slices. Toss fish, cornstarch, vegetable oil, ½ teaspoon salt, the soy sauce, sesame oil and white pepper in 1-quart glass or plastic bowl. Cover and refrigerate 30 minutes.

Remove core from lettuce; cut lettuce into 8 pieces. Heat chicken broth to boiling in 3-quart saucepan. Add lettuce and 1 teaspoon salt; heat to boiling. Stir in fish. Heat to boiling; remove from heat. Stir in green onion.

Oriental Seafood Soup

1 small unpared cucumber
2 cans (10¾ ounces each) condensed
* chicken broth*
2⅓ cups water
1 tablespoon soy sauce
⅛ teaspoon ground ginger
Dash of pepper
2 ounces uncooked vermicelli
½ pound firm fish fillets, cut into ½-inch
* slices*
1 can (4½ ounces) tiny shrimp, rinsed
* and drained*
1 cup sliced mushrooms* (about 3 ounces)
5 cups torn spinach (about 4 ounces)
¼ cup sliced green onions (with tops)

Cut cucumber lengthwise into halves; remove seeds. Cut each half crosswise into thin slices. Heat chicken broth, water, soy sauce, ginger and pepper to boiling in 3-quart saucepan; stir in vermicelli. Heat to boiling; cook uncovered just until vermicelli is tender, about 4 minutes. Stir in cucumber, fish, shrimp and mushrooms. Heat to boiling; reduce heat. Simmer uncovered until fish flakes easily with fork, about 1 minute. Stir in spinach until wilted. Sprinkle each serving with green onions.

*1 can (4 ounces) mushroom stems and pieces, drained, can be substituted for the fresh mushrooms.

Crabmeat-Vegetable Soup

4 SERVINGS

1 medium onion, chopped (about ½ cup)
1 clove garlic, crushed
1 tablespoon margarine or butter
1 large tomato, peeled and chopped
3 cups Fish Broth (page 103)
2 tablespoons snipped parsley
½ teaspoon salt
3 drops red pepper sauce
4 new potatoes, cut into halves
1 package (10 ounces) frozen whole kernel
   corn
1½ cups cooked crabmeat

Cook and stir onion and garlic in margarine in 3-quart saucepan until onion is tender. Stir in tomato; cook 2 minutes. Stir in broth, parsley, salt, pepper sauce, potatoes and corn. Heat to boiling; reduce heat. Cover and simmer until potatoes are tender, about 10 minutes. Stir in crabmeat. Heat 2 minutes.

Gorgonzola–White Bean Soup

4 SERVINGS

1 medium onion, chopped (about ½ cup)
1 medium stalk celery, chopped (about
   ½ cup)
1 medium carrot, chopped (about ½ cup)
1 tablespoon margarine or butter
3 cups chicken broth
1 medium leek, cut into ¼-inch slices
   (about 1 cup)
½ cup dried white beans (about 4 ounces)
1 cup milk
1 ounce Gorgonzola cheese, crumbled

Cook onion, celery and carrot in margarine in 3-quart saucepan over medium heat until onion is tender, about 3 minutes. Stir in chicken broth, leek and beans. Heat to boiling; boil 2 minutes. Reduce heat and simmer until beans are tender, about 2 hours. (Add water during cooking if liquid does not cover beans.) Stir in milk.

Place 1 cup of the soup in blender container or workbowl of food processor fitted with steel blade. Cover and blend on high speed until of uniform consistency, about 30 seconds; stir into remaining soup mixture. Stir in cheese until melted.

Vegetable-Cheese Soup with Popcorn

4 SERVINGS

2 tablespoons margarine or butter
2 tablespoons all-purpose flour
1 cup chicken broth
2 medium carrots, coarsely chopped
   (about 1 cup)
2 medium stalks celery, coarsely chopped
   (about 1 cup)
1 medium onion, chopped (about ½ cup)
1 can (15 ounces) evaporated milk
½ teaspoon Worcestershire sauce
1 cup shredded sharp Cheddar cheese
   (4 ounces)
1 cup popped popcorn

Heat margarine in 3-quart saucepan over low heat until melted. Stir in flour. Cook over low heat until mixture is smooth and bubbly, stirring constantly; remove from heat. Stir in chicken broth, carrots, celery and onion. Heat to boiling; boil and stir 1 minute. Reduce heat; cover and simmer until vegetables are crisp-tender, about 8 minutes. Stir in milk, Worcestershire sauce and cheese. Stir constantly until hot and cheese has melted, 2 to 3 minutes longer (do not boil). Top with popcorn.

Quick Tomato-Yogurt Soup

4 SERVINGS

1 can (10¾ ounces) condensed tomato
   soup
⅔ cup plain yogurt

Mix soup and yogurt in 1-quart saucepan. Heat over medium heat, stirring constantly, until hot.

Avocado Broth

10 SERVINGS

2 cans (10½ ounces each) condensed beef
   broth
2 broth cans water
3 to 4 drops red pepper sauce
2 tablespoons lemon juice
1 large ripe avocado,* thinly sliced

Heat beef broth, water, red pepper sauce and lemon juice just to boiling. Add avocado.

*Choose an avocado that is still somewhat firm, without any soft spots. Dip avocado slices into lemon juice if not adding them to the broth immediately; it will keep them from discoloring.

Following pages: Gorgonzola—White Bean Soup and Mini Ham and Turkey Sandwiches (page 66)

Shredded Cabbage Soup

2 medium onions, thinly sliced
3 tablespoons bacon fat, margarine or
    butter
2 cans (10½ ounces each) condensed beef
    broth
2 broth cans water
1 small head green cabbage, coarsely
    shredded (5 cups)
2 medium carrots, sliced
2 medium potatoes, cubed
1 stalk celery (with leaves), sliced
2 medium tomatoes, coarsely chopped
1 teaspoon salt
Freshly ground pepper
Dairy sour cream
Dill weed or parsley

Cook and stir onions in bacon fat in Dutch oven until tender. Add beef broth, water, cabbage, carrots, potatoes and celery. Heat to boiling; reduce heat. Cover and simmer until vegetables are tender, about 20 minutes. Stir in tomatoes, salt and pepper. Simmer uncovered about 10 minutes. Top each serving with sour cream. Garnish with dill weed.

Easy Spinach Soup

2½ cups water
1 tablespoon instant beef or chicken
    bouillon
1 package (10 ounces) frozen chopped
    spinach
1 can (4 ounces) mushroom stems and
    pieces, undrained
1 jar (2 ounces) sliced pimientos, drained
½ teaspoon garlic salt
Dash of dried rosemary leaves
4 tablespoons plain yogurt

Heat water, bouillon (dry) and spinach to boiling; break up spinach with fork. Cover and cook until tender, about 3 minutes. Stir in mushrooms, pimientos, garlic salt and rosemary; heat until hot. Garnish with yogurt.

· 2 ·
COLD SOUPS

Fresh Fruit Soup

3 tablespoons sugar
3 tablespoons cornstarch
1/8 teaspoon salt
1 1/4 cups medium red wine
1 cup water
1 1/2 cups cranberry juice cocktail
3 cups fresh fruit, such as strawberries,
   blueberries, bananas, seedless green
   grapes, cantaloupe, pitted cherries

Mix sugar, cornstarch and salt in 3-quart saucepan; stir in wine and water. Heat to boiling, stirring constantly. Boil and stir 1 minute. Remove from heat; stir in cranberry juice. Cover loosely and refrigerate until chilled.

Stir in fruit. Top each serving with spoonful of sour cream or whipped cream, if desired.

Following pages: Fresh Fruit Soup, left, and Cream of Cherry Soup, right (page 22)

Cream of Cherry Soup

1 pound dark sweet cherries, pitted and
   cut into fourths
1/2 cup sugar
3 cups water
1 teaspoon lemon juice
1/4 teaspoon cardamom seed
2 tablespoons cornstarch
2 tablespoons water
1/2 cup dairy sour cream
1/3 cup dry red wine, chilled
8 whole dark sweet cherries

Heat cut-up cherries, sugar, 3 cups water, the lemon juice and cardamom seed to boiling. Reduce heat; simmer uncovered until cherries are tender, about 10 minutes. Pour half the cherry mixture into blender container. Cover and blend on high speed until smooth. Repeat with remaining mixture. Return to saucepan; heat to boiling. Mix cornstarch and 2 tablespoons water; stir gradually into cherries. Continue boiling, stirring constantly, until soup thickens and becomes clear, about 2 minutes. Cover and refrigerate until chilled, at least 4 hours. Just before serving, stir in sour cream and wine. Garnish each serving with whole cherry.

Dried Fruit Soup

2 packages (about 6 ounces each) mixed
   dried fruit, such as prunes, apricots,
   peaches, pears, raisins (2 cups)
1/2 cup sugar
1 1/2 cups water
1 1/2 cups grape juice or cranberry juice
   cocktail
2 tablespoons quick-cooking tapioca
1/4 teaspoon salt
2 or 3 thin slices lemon, if desired
3-inch cinnamon stick
1 can (8 ounces) pitted dark sweet
   cherries, undrained

Heat all ingredients except cherries to boiling in 3-quart saucepan, stirring occasionally. Reduce heat; cover and simmer until fruit is tender, 30 to 40 minutes. Stir in cherries and heat. Serve warm or refrigerate until chilled.

Cold Cucumber Soup

2 medium cucumbers
1½ cups plain yogurt
½ teaspoon salt
¾ teaspoon snipped fresh mint or
   ¼ teaspoon dried mint flakes
⅛ teaspoon white pepper

Cut 7 thin slices from cucumber; reserve. Cut remaining cucumber into ¾-inch chunks. Place half of the cucumber chunks and ¼ cup of the yogurt in blender container. Cover and blend on high speed until smooth. Add remaining cucumber, the salt, mint and white pepper. Cover and blend until smooth. Add remaining yogurt; cover and blend on low speed until smooth. Cover and refrigerate until chilled, at least 1 hour. Garnish with reserved cucumber slices.

Cold Potato Soup

1 large onion, chopped (about 1 cup)
1 medium stalk celery, chopped (about
   ½ cup)
1 tablespoon margarine or butter
4 medium potatoes, chopped
2 cans (10¾ ounces each) condensed
   chicken broth
2 cups half-and-half
1 teaspoon salt
¼ teaspoon pepper
1¾ to 2 cups half-and-half

Cook and stir onion and celery in margarine in 3-quart saucepan until onion is tender, about 5 minutes. Add potatoes and broth. Heat to boiling; reduce heat. Cover and simmer until potatoes are tender, 15 to 20 minutes.

Pour half of the potato mixture into blender container. Cover and blend on medium speed until mixture is smooth, about 45 seconds. Repeat with remaining potato mixture. Stir in 2 cups half-and-half, the salt and pepper. Cover and refrigerate at least 6 hours but no longer than 24 hours.

At serving time, stir in enough half-and-half until desired consistency.

Chilled Yogurt-Vegetable Soup

1/4 cup margarine or butter
1 cup thinly sliced mushrooms
4 medium carrots, shredded
2 small zucchini, shredded
1/3 cup finely chopped onion
1 teaspoon dried dill weed
4 cups chicken broth
1 package (10 ounces) frozen green peas
2 cups plain yogurt

Heat margarine in 4-quart saucepan over medium heat until melted. Stir in mushrooms, carrots, zucchini, onion and dill weed. Cover and cook 2½ minutes; stir once. Cover and cook until vegetables are crisp-tender, about 2½ minutes longer; add broth and peas. Heat to boiling over high heat; remove from heat. Pour into bowl; cool completely. Stir in yogurt; cover and refrigerate until chilled. Sprinkle with salt and pepper, if desired.

Easy Borsch

1 can (16 ounces) shoestring beets,
   undrained
1 can (10½ ounces) condensed beef broth
1 cup shredded cabbage
2 tablespoons finely chopped onion
1 teaspoon sugar
1 teaspoon lemon juice
Dairy sour cream

Heat beets, broth, cabbage, onion and sugar to boiling; reduce heat. Simmer uncovered 5 minutes. Stir in lemon juice. Serve hot, or refrigerate until chilled. Top each serving with spoonful of sour cream.

Gazpacho

3 cups tomato juice
2 beef bouillon cubes
2 tomatoes, chopped
1/2 cup chopped cucumber
1/4 cup chopped green pepper
1 small onion, chopped (about 1/4 cup)
1/4 cup wine vinegar
2 tablespoons vegetable oil
1/2 teaspoon salt
1 teaspoon Worcestershire sauce
6 drops red pepper sauce
Garnishes (herbed croutons and about 2/3
  cup each of chopped cucumber, tomato,
  green pepper and onion)

Heat tomato juice to boiling. Add bouillon cubes; stir until dissolved. Stir in remaining ingredients except garnishes. Refrigerate several hours. Serve with garnishes.

Guacamole Soup

4 SERVINGS

2 medium avocados
1 1/2 cups water
1 cup milk
2 tablespoons lemon juice
2 teaspoons seasoned salt
Dash of red pepper sauce
1 medium tomato, chopped

Cut avocados lengthwise into fourths; remove pits and peel. Place avocados, water and milk in blender container. Cover and blend until smooth. Stir in remaining ingredients. Refrigerate until chilled. Garnish each serving with lemon slices, if desired.

· 3 ·

HEARTY SOUPS

French-style Chicken Soup

2½- to 3-pound broiler-fryer chicken,
  cut up
2 tablespoons vegetable oil
2 large onions, thinly sliced and
  separated into rings
2 cloves garlic, finely chopped
1 cup water
1 cup dry white wine or apple juice
1 tablespoon sugar
1 teaspoon salt
1 teaspoon dried thyme leaves
¼ teaspoon pepper
1 can (16 ounces) whole tomatoes,
  undrained
1 can (10¾ ounces) condensed chicken
  broth
1 medium green pepper, cut into ¼-inch
  strips
8 slices French bread, toasted
Snipped parsley

Remove skin and any excess fat from chicken pieces. Heat oil in Dutch oven. Cook chicken in oil until brown on all sides; remove chicken from pan. Cook and stir onions and garlic in same pan until onion is tender. Return chicken to pan; add water, wine, sugar, salt, thyme, pepper, tomatoes and broth; break up tomatoes with fork. Heat to boiling; reduce heat. Cover and simmer until chicken is done, about 1 hour.

Skim fat from chicken mixture. Add green pepper. Heat to boiling; reduce heat. Cover and simmer just until green pepper is tender, about 10 minutes. Place a slice of French bread in each serving bowl. Spoon chicken and broth over bread. Sprinkle with parsley.

Chicken Gumbo

3- to 4-pound broiler-fryer chicken,
    cut up
2 cups water or chicken broth
1 cup chopped celery tops
2 teaspoons salt
1 medium onion, sliced
1 clove garlic, crushed
1 large bay leaf
1 medium onion, chopped (about ½ cup)
1 small green pepper, chopped (about
    ½ cup)
2 tablespoons margarine or butter
¼ cup snipped parsley
½ teaspoon red pepper sauce
1 can (28 ounces) whole tomatoes,
    undrained
1½ cups sliced fresh or frozen okra
⅓ cup uncooked long grain rice
Dash of pepper
1½ teaspoons filé powder

Remove any excess fat from chicken. Heat chicken, giblets (except liver), neck, water, celery tops, salt, sliced onion, garlic and bay leaf to boiling; reduce heat. Cover and simmer until thickest pieces of chicken are done, about 45 minutes.

Remove chicken from broth; cool chicken 10 minutes. Remove chicken from bones and skin; cut chicken into bite-size pieces. Skim fat from broth; strain broth. Place broth and chicken in Dutch oven.

Cook and stir chopped onion and green pepper in margarine until onion is tender. Stir onion mixture, parsley, pepper sauce and tomatoes into chicken and broth; break up tomatoes with fork. Heat to boiling; reduce heat. Simmer uncovered 15 minutes.

Stir in okra, rice and pepper. Heat to boiling; reduce heat. Cover and simmer until rice is done, about 15 minutes. Remove from heat; stir in filé powder. Remove bay leaf; serve. (Soup can be prepared ahead; stir in filé powder after reheating.)

Calico Bean Soup

8 cups water
Bean Soup Mix (below)
2 medium carrots, chopped (about 1 cup)
2 stalks celery, chopped (about 1 cup)
2 pounds smoked ham shanks, ham hocks
    or 1 ham bone

Heat water and Bean Soup Mix to boiling in Dutch oven; boil 2 minutes. Remove from heat; cover and let stand 1 hour.

Stir in carrots and celery; add ham shanks. Heat to boiling; reduce heat. Cover and simmer until beans are tender, about 2 hours. Skim fat if necessary.

Remove ham shanks; remove ham from bone. Trim excess fat from ham; cut ham into ½-inch pieces. Stir ham into soup. Heat until hot.

BEAN SOUP MIX

2 cups mixed dried beans (⅓ cup each of
    yellow split peas, green split peas,
    lima beans, pinto beans, kidney beans
    and great northern beans)
¼ cup instant minced onion
2 teaspoons instant chicken bouillon
¼ teaspoon ground cumin
¼ teaspoon garlic powder

Combine all ingredients.

Do-ahead Tip: Prepare several packages of Bean Soup Mix and store in plastic bag or airtight container in a cool, dry place. Use 1 soup mix package for each recipe of Calico Bean Soup.

Beans and Franks Soup

3 carrots, sliced
2 medium onions, chopped
1 clove garlic, finely chopped
2 tablespoons margarine or butter
1 can (28 ounces) baked beans in brown
    sugar sauce
1 can (12 ounces) eight-vegetable juice or
    tomato juice
6 frankfurters, cut into 1-inch slices
1 teaspoon Worcestershire sauce
Shredded American or Cheddar cheese

Cook carrots, onions and garlic in margarine in 3-quart saucepan, stirring frequently, until carrots are crisp-tender.

Stir in remaining ingredients except cheese. Heat over medium heat, stirring occasionally, until hot. Sprinkle with cheese.

BEANS AND FRANKS SOUP WITH VEGETABLES: Prepare as directed above except omit carrots. Stir in 1 package (10 ounces) frozen mixed vegetables with the beans.

Beef and Barley Soup

5 slices bacon
1-pound beef chuck roast or steak, cut
　　into 1-inch pieces
2 large onions, chopped (about 2 cups)
2 cloves garlic, finely chopped
2 cups water
1/4 cup barley
1 1/2 teaspoons paprika
1 teaspoon salt
1/4 teaspoon caraway seed
1/8 teaspoon dried marjoram leaves
2 cans (10 1/2 ounces each) condensed beef
　　broth
3 medium potatoes, cut into 1/2-inch pieces
　　(about 3 cups)
2 medium carrots, sliced (about 1 cup)
2 medium stalks celery, sliced (about
　　1 cup)
1 can (16 ounces) stewed tomatoes
1 package (10 ounces) frozen green peas,
　　broken apart
1 can (4 ounces) mushroom stems and
　　pieces, undrained

Fry bacon in Dutch oven over medium heat until crisp. Remove bacon; drain and reserve. Cook and stir beef, onions and garlic in bacon fat in Dutch oven until beef is brown. Stir in water, barley, paprika, salt, caraway seed, marjoram and broth. Heat to boiling; reduce heat. Cover and simmer 1 1/2 hours.

Stir in potatoes, carrots, celery, tomatoes, peas and mushrooms. Heat to boiling; reduce heat. Cover and simmer until vegetables are tender, 30 to 40 minutes. Crumble bacon; sprinkle over soup.

Following pages: Calico Bean Soup

Chunky Beef-Noodle Soup

4 SERVINGS

*1 pound beef boneless round steak, cut
    into ¾-inch pieces*
1 large onion, chopped (about 1 cup)
2 cloves garlic, finely chopped
1 tablespoon vegetable oil
2 cups water
2 teaspoons chili powder
1½ teaspoons salt
½ teaspoon dried oregano leaves
*1 can (16 ounces) whole tomatoes,
    undrained*
1 can (10½ ounces) condensed beef broth
*2 ounces uncooked egg noodles (about
    1 cup)*
*1 medium green pepper, coarsely chopped
    (about 1 cup)*
¼ cup snipped parsley

Cook and stir beef, onion and garlic in oil in Dutch oven until beef is brown, about 15 minutes. Stir in water, chili powder, salt, oregano, tomatoes and broth; break up tomatoes with fork. Heat to boiling; reduce heat. Cover and simmer until beef is tender, 1½ to 2 hours.

Skim excess fat from soup. Stir noodles and green pepper into soup. Heat to boiling; reduce heat. Simmer uncovered until noodles are tender, about 10 minutes. Stir in parsley.

Philadelphia Pepper Pot Soup

8 SERVINGS

½ teaspoon whole black peppercorns
6 whole cloves
1 bay leaf
2 pounds veal shanks, cracked
7 cups water
1 medium onion, chopped
½ medium red bell pepper, chopped
2 tablespoons snipped parsley
*1 tablespoon snipped fresh or 1 teaspoon
    dried marjoram*
1½ teaspoons salt
*1 teaspoon snipped fresh or ¼ teaspoon
    dried thyme*
¼ teaspoon crushed red pepper
*2 medium potatoes, pared and cut into
    ½-inch cubes*

Tie peppercorns, cloves and bay leaf in small cheesecloth bag. Place veal shanks, water, cheesecloth bag and remaining ingredients except potatoes in Dutch oven. Heat to boiling; reduce heat. Cover and simmer 2 hours. Discard cheesecloth bag.

Remove shanks from broth; cool shanks about 10 minutes or just until cool enough to handle. Remove veal from bones; cut veal into ½-inch pieces. Skim fat from broth. Stir veal and potatoes into broth. Heat to boiling; reduce heat. Cover and simmer about 15 minutes or until potatoes are tender.

Creole-style Sausage-Potato Soup

1½ pounds large smoked sausage links,
  cut into 3- to 4-inch pieces
2 tablespoons sugar
1 teaspoon salt
2 medium carrots, thinly sliced (about
  1 cup)
2 medium stalks celery, sliced (about
  1 cup)
1 envelope (about 1½ ounces) onion soup
  mix
6 cups boiling water
1 can (28 ounces) whole tomatoes,
  undrained
¼ teaspoon oregano
¼ teaspoon red pepper sauce
1 package (6 ounces) hash brown potato
  mix with onions

Place sausage, sugar, salt, carrots, celery and onion soup mix in Dutch oven; add boiling water. Cover and simmer 10 minutes. Add tomatoes; break up with fork. Stir in oregano, pepper sauce and potato mix. Heat to boiling; reduce heat. Cover and simmer until vegetables are tender, 30 to 40 minutes.

Cheddar Cheese Soup

1 small onion, chopped
1 medium stalk celery, thinly sliced
2 tablespoons margarine or butter
2 tablespoons all-purpose flour
¼ teaspoon pepper
¼ teaspoon dry mustard
1 can (10¾ ounces) condensed chicken
  broth
1 cup milk
2 cups shredded Cheddar cheese
  (8 ounces)
Paprika

Cover and simmer onion and celery in margarine in 2-quart saucepan until onion is tender, about 5 minutes. Stir in flour, pepper and mustard. Cook over low heat, stirring constantly until smooth and bubbly; remove from heat. Add chicken broth and milk. Heat to boiling over medium heat, stirring constantly. Boil and stir 1 minute. Stir in cheese; heat over low heat, stirring occasionally, just until cheese is melted (do not boil). Sprinkle soup with paprika.

Following pages: Muffuletta (page 69) and Creole-style Sausage-Potato Soup

Beer and Cheese Soup

1 medium onion, chopped (about 1/2 cup)
2 tablespoons margarine or butter
1/2 cup finely chopped carrots
1/2 cup finely chopped celery
1 bottle or can (12 ounces) beer
2 cups chicken broth
1 teaspoon salt
1 teaspoon ground cumin
1/4 teaspoon ground nutmeg
Dash of ground cloves
Dash of pepper
1 cup dairy sour cream
4 ounces Cheddar or Monterey Jack
   cheese, cut into 1/4-inch cubes (about
   1 cup)

Cook and stir onion in margarine in 2-quart saucepan until tender. Stir in carrots, celery and beer. Heat to boiling; reduce heat. Cover and simmer 10 minutes. Stir in chicken broth, salt, cumin, nutmeg, cloves and pepper. Heat to boiling; reduce heat. Cover and simmer 30 minutes. Remove from heat; stir in sour cream. Sprinkle with cheese.

·4·
CHOWDERS AND BISQUES

Chicken and Corn Chowder

3- to 3½-pound broiler-fryer chicken,
   cut up
6 cups water
1 medium onion, sliced
3 medium stalks celery (with leaves),
   finely chopped (about 1½ cups)
1 medium carrot, chopped (about ½ cup)
2 teaspoons salt
1 can (17 ounces) cream-style corn
2 hard-cooked eggs, finely chopped
Egg Rivels (below)

Remove any excess fat from chicken. Place chicken, giblets (except liver) and neck in Dutch oven. Add water, onion, celery, carrot and salt; heat to boiling. Skim foam from broth; reduce heat. Cover and simmer about 1½ hours or until thickest pieces of chicken are done.

Remove chicken from broth; cool chicken about 10 minutes or just until cool enough to handle. Remove chicken from bones and skin; cut chicken into small pieces. Skim fat from broth; return chicken to broth. Stir in corn and eggs. Heat to boiling; reduce heat. Sprinkle with Egg Rivels; stir into soup. Simmer uncovered 10 minutes.

EGG RIVELS

1 cup all-purpose flour
¼ teaspoon salt
1 egg

Mix all ingredients until mixture looks like cornmeal.

Chicken-Broccoli Chowder

6 SERVINGS

2 cups chicken broth
1/3 cup chopped onion
1 package (10 ounces) frozen chopped
   broccoli
1 1/3 cups mashed potato mix
2 cups cut-up cooked chicken
2 cups shredded Swiss cheese (about
   8 ounces)
2 cups milk
1/2 teaspoon salt

Heat chicken broth, onion and broccoli to boiling in 3-quart saucepan. Reduce heat; cover and simmer 5 minutes. Stir in potato mix until well blended. Stir in remaining ingredients. Heat over low heat, stirring occasionally, until hot and cheese is melted, about 5 minutes.

Sausage Chowder

4 SERVINGS

1 package (12 ounces) smoked sausage
   links, cut into 1/2-inch slices
1 small green pepper, chopped (about
   1/2 cup)
1 small onion, chopped (about 1/4 cup)
1 tablespoon margarine or butter
2/3 cup milk
1 can (16 1/2 ounces) cream-style corn
1 can (10 3/4 ounces) condensed cream of
   potato soup

Cook and stir sausage, green pepper and onion in margarine in 3-quart saucepan over medium heat until sausage is brown. Stir in remaining ingredients; heat just until hot (do not boil).

Manhattan Clam Chowder

5 SERVINGS

1/4 cup finely cut-up lean salt pork or
bacon or margarine or butter
1 small onion, finely chopped (about
1/4 cup)
2 cans (6 1/2 ounces each) minced or whole
clams, drained (reserve liquid)*
2 cups finely chopped potatoes
1 cup water
1/3 cup chopped celery
2 teaspoons snipped parsley
1 teaspoon salt
1/4 teaspoon dried thyme leaves
1/8 teaspoon pepper
1 can (16 ounces) whole tomatoes,
undrained

Cook and stir salt pork and onion in Dutch oven until pork is crisp and onion is tender. Drain clams, reserving liquid. Stir clam liquid, potatoes, water and celery into onion and pork. Cover and cook until potatoes are tender, about 10 minutes. Stir in clams, and the remaining ingredients. Break up tomatoes with fork. Heat to boiling, stirring occasionally.

*1 pint shucked fresh clams with liquid can be substituted for the canned clams. Chop clams and add with the potatoes.

New England Clam Chowder

4 SERVINGS

1/4 cup cut-up bacon or lean salt pork
1 medium onion, chopped (about 1/2 cup)
2 cans (6 1/2 ounces each) minced or whole
clams, drained (reserve liquid)*
1 cup finely chopped potato
1/2 teaspoon salt
Dash of pepper
2 cups milk

Cook and stir bacon and onion in 2-quart saucepan until bacon is crisp and onion is tender. Add enough water, if necessary, to reserved clam liquid to measure 1 cup. Stir clams, liquid, potato, salt and pepper into onion mixture. Heat to boiling. Cover and cook until potato is tender, about 15 minutes. Stir in milk. Heat, stirring occasionally, just until hot (do not boil).

*1 pint shucked fresh clams with liquid can be substituted for the canned clams. Chop clams and add with the potatoes.

Following pages: Manhattan Clam Chowder, left, and New England Clam Chowder, right

Quick Ham and Cauliflower Chowder

4 SERVINGS

2¹/₂ cups water
¹/₂ cup chopped cauliflower
¹/₈ teaspoon dry mustard
Dash of pepper
1 package (5.25 ounces) scalloped potato
  mix
1 can (10³/₄ ounces) condensed chicken
  broth
1 cup diced fully cooked smoked ham
1 cup half-and-half

Mix water, cauliflower, mustard, pepper, potatoes, Sauce Mix and broth in 3-quart saucepan. Heat to boiling, stirring frequently; reduce heat. Cover and simmer, stirring occasionally, until potatoes are tender, 25 minutes. Stir in ham and half-and-half. Cook uncovered just until hot, about 5 minutes longer (do not boil). Garnish with snipped parsley, if desired.

Cheesy Vegetable Chowder

7 SERVINGS

2 cups water
1 teaspoon salt
3 medium carrots, sliced (about 1 cup)
2 stalks celery, chopped (about ¹/₂ cup)
1 small onion, chopped (about ¹/₄ cup)
¹/₂ cup margarine or butter
¹/₂ cup all-purpose flour
¹/₂ teaspoon pepper
2 cups milk
1 can (8 ounces) whole kernel corn,
  drained, or 1 cup frozen whole kernel
  corn
1 can (8¹/₂ ounces) green peas, drained,
  or 1 cup frozen green peas
1 can (4 ounces) mushroom stems and
  pieces, drained
6 slices bacon, crisply fried and crumbled
4 ounces Swiss or American cheese, cut
  into ¹/₂-inch cubes

Heat water to boiling in 3-quart saucepan. Stir in salt, carrots, celery and onion. Heat to boiling; reduce heat. Cover and simmer until vegetables are tender, about 10 minutes. Heat margarine in 2-quart saucepan over low heat until melted; stir in flour and pepper. Heat to boiling over medium heat, stirring constantly. Remove from heat; gradually stir in milk. Heat to boiling, stirring constantly; boil and stir 1 minute. Stir milk mixture, corn, peas, mushrooms and bacon into carrot mixture; heat until hot. Stir in cheese; heat until cheese begins to melt. Top each serving with croutons, if desired.

Apple and Squash Bisque

6 SERVINGS

*1 can (14½ ounces) ready-to-serve
chicken broth*
1 butternut squash (about 2 pounds),
pared and cubed*
½ cup chopped onion
2 cups applesauce
½ teaspoon ground ginger
¼ teaspoon salt
1 cup dairy sour cream

Heat chicken broth to boiling in 3-quart saucepan; add squash and onion. Cover and heat to boiling; reduce heat. Boil 15 to 20 minutes or until squash is tender. Stir in applesauce, ginger and salt. Place ⅓ to ½ of the mixture at a time in blender container or workbowl of food processor fitted with steel blade. Cover and blend until smooth. Return soup to saucepan; stir in sour cream. Heat over low heat, stirring occasionally, until hot. Garnish with additional sour cream and sprinkle with poppy seed, if desired.

*2 packages (10 ounces each) frozen squash, thawed, can be substituted for the butternut squash.

TO MICROWAVE: Place chicken broth, squash and onion in 3-quart microwavable casserole. Cover tightly and microwave on high 13 to 16 minutes, stirring after 5 minutes, until tender. Stir in applesauce, ginger and salt. Blend as directed above. Return soup to casserole; stir in sour cream. Microwave uncovered on medium-high (70%) 6 to 8 minutes, stirring every 2 minutes, until hot.

Fresh Tomato Bisque

1 large onion, chopped (about 1 cup)
1 medium stalk celery, chopped (about
    ½ cup)
1 tablespoon snipped fresh or 1 teaspoon
    dried basil
1 clove garlic, finely chopped
2 tablespoons margarine or butter
1½ teaspoons instant chicken bouillon
1 teaspoon sugar
6 large tomatoes, peeled, seeded and
    chopped (about 3 pounds)
1 tablespoon lemon juice
Freshly ground pepper

Cook and stir onion, celery, basil and garlic in margarine in 3-quart saucepan about 5 minutes or until onion is tender. Stir in bouillon (dry), sugar and tomatoes. Heat to boiling; reduce heat. Cover and simmer about 10 minutes or until tomatoes are tender. Place half of the mixture in workbowl of food processor fitted with steel blade or blender container. Cover and process until smooth. Return to saucepan; heat through if necessary. Stir in lemon juice; sprinkle with pepper. Garnish with thin pats of butter, if desired.

Shrimp Bisque

1 teaspoon grated onion
1 tablespoon margarine or butter
1 tablespoon all-purpose flour
2 teaspoons snipped parsley
¾ teaspoon salt
⅛ teaspoon celery salt
⅛ teaspoon pepper
2 cups milk
1 cup chicken broth or water
2 cans (4¼ ounces each) shrimp, drained
    (reserve liquid)

Cook and stir onion in margarine over low heat. Stir in flour, parsley, salt, celery salt and pepper. Cook, stirring constantly, until mixture is smooth and bubbly. Remove from heat; stir in milk and chicken broth. Heat to boiling, stirring constantly. Boil and stir 1 minute. Stir in shrimp and liquid.

Wild Rice–Chicken Soup

⅓ cup uncooked wild rice
4 cups chicken broth
½ cup sliced mushrooms
¼ cup chopped celery
1 small onion, chopped (about ¼ cup)
1 clove garlic, crushed
½ teaspoon salt
¼ teaspoon pepper
¼ cup margarine or butter
⅓ cup all-purpose flour
1 cup cut-up cooked chicken
1 cup whipping cream
2 tablespoons dry white wine

Wash wild rice by placing in wire strainer; run cold water through it, lifting rice with fingers to clean thoroughly. Heat rice and chicken broth to boiling, stirring once or twice; reduce heat. Cover and simmer until tender, 40 to 50 minutes.

Cook and stir mushrooms, celery, onion, garlic, salt and pepper in margarine in 3-quart saucepan until celery is tender, about 6 minutes. Stir in flour. Cook over low heat, stirring constantly, until mixture is bubbly; remove from heat. Stir in cut-up chicken and chicken broth with rice. Heat to boiling, stirring constantly. Stir in cream and wine; heat just until hot (do not boil).

Summer Vegetable Soup

2 cups water
1 cup cut fresh or frozen green beans
¾ cup fresh or frozen green peas
¼ small cauliflower, separated into
  flowerets
2 small carrots, sliced
1 medium potato, cubed
2 ounces spinach, cut up (about 2 cups)
2 cups milk
2 tablespoons all-purpose flour
¼ cup whipping cream
1½ teaspoons salt
⅛ teaspoon pepper
Snipped dill weed or parsley

Heat water, beans, peas, cauliflower, carrots and potato to boiling in 3-quart saucepan; reduce heat. Cover and simmer until vegetables are crisp-tender, 10 to 15 minutes.

Add spinach; cook uncovered about 1 minute. Mix ¼ cup of the milk and the flour; gradually stir into vegetable mixture. Boil and stir 1 minute. Stir in remaining milk, the cream, salt and pepper. Heat just until hot (do not boil). Garnish each serving with dill weed.

Following pages: Swiss Cheese and Vegetables in Pita Breads (page 80) and Fresh Tomato Bisque

Creamy Cauliflower Soup

8 SERVINGS

2 cups water
1 medium head cauliflower (about
    2 pounds), broken into flowerets (about
    6 cups)
1 large stalk celery, chopped (about
    ¾ cup)
1 medium onion, chopped (about ½ cup)
1 tablespoon lemon juice
2 tablespoons margarine or butter
2 tablespoons all-purpose flour
2½ cups water
1 tablespoon instant chicken bouillon
¾ teaspoon salt
⅛ teaspoon pepper
Dash of ground nutmeg
½ cup whipping cream

Heat 2 cups water to boiling in 3-quart sauce-pan. Add cauliflower, celery, onion and lemon juice. Cover; heat to boiling. Cook until tender, about 10 minutes; do not drain. Place in blender container. Cover and blend until uniform consistency.

Heat margarine in 3-quart saucepan over low heat until melted. Stir in flour. Cook, stirring constantly, until mixture is smooth and bubbly.

Remove from heat; stir in 2½ cups water. Heat to boiling, stirring constantly. Boil and stir 1 minute. Stir in cauliflower mixture, bouillon (dry), salt, pepper and nutmeg. Heat just to boiling. Stir in cream; heat just until hot (do not boil). Serve with grated cheese, if desired.

Quick Creamy Potato Soup

8 SERVINGS

3½ cups milk
2 tablespoons margarine or butter
2 tablespoons finely chopped onion or
    1 tablespoon instant minced onion
1½ teaspoons salt
¼ teaspoon celery salt
⅛ teaspoon pepper
1⅓ cups mashed potato mix
Paprika
Snipped parsley

Heat milk, margarine, onion, salt, celery salt and pepper to scalding in 2-quart saucepan. Stir in potato mix; continue cooking, stirring constantly, until smooth. (Soup should be consistency of whipping cream.) Garnish each serving with paprika and parsley.

·5·
PARTY SANDWICHES

Pinwheels

1 loaf sandwich bread, unsliced
Margarine or butter, softened
Spreads (below)

Remove entire crust from bread. Cut loaf horizontally into ¼-inch slices. Spread each slice with 2 tablespoons margarine and ½ cup of one of the spreads. Cut each slice in half crosswise. Roll up as for jelly roll, beginning at narrow end. Secure with wooden picks. Wrap and chill. Slice ½ inch thick.

CREAM CHEESE SPREAD

2 packages (3 ounces each) cream cheese, softened
½ cup margarine or butter, softened
1 teaspoon anchovy paste
1 teaspoon instant minced onion
1 teaspoon dry mustard
2 teaspoons paprika

Mix all ingredients.

GOLDEN SPREAD

2 cups shredded Cheddar cheese (about 8 ounces)
1 package (3 ounces) cream cheese, softened
¼ cup mayonnaise or salad dressing
½ teaspoon Worcestershire sauce
⅛ teaspoon onion powder
⅛ teaspoon garlic powder
⅛ teaspoon celery salt

Mix all ingredients.

Following pages: Pinwheels, Watercress Triangles (page 57) and Cucumber Sandwiches (page 57)

Sandwich Loaf

Fillings (below and right)
1 loaf (1½ pounds) unsliced sandwich bread
Margarine or butter, softened
2 packages (8 ounces each) cream cheese, softened
½ cup half-and-half

Prepare Fillings. Trim crust from loaf; cut loaf horizontally into 4 equal slices. Spread 3 slices with margarine. Place 1 slice on serving plate and spread evenly with Shrimp Salad Filling. Top with second slice and spread evenly with Cream Cheese–Pecan Filling. Top with third slice and spread evenly with Chicken-Bacon Filling. Top with unbuttered bread slice.

Mix cream cheese and half-and-half until smooth and of spreading consistency. Frost sides and top of loaf with cream cheese mixture. Refrigerate until set, about 30 minutes. Cover loaf and refrigerate at least 2½ hours but no longer than 24 hours. Garnish with slices of hard-cooked egg, slices of ripe olives and thin strips of green onion tops, if desired.

SHRIMP SALAD FILLING

2 tablespoons finely chopped celery
⅛ teaspoon salt
Dash of pepper
3 tablespoons mayonnaise or salad dressing
1 tablespoon lemon juice
1 hard-cooked egg, finely chopped
1 can (4¼ ounces) broken shrimp, rinsed and drained

Mix all ingredients.

CREAM CHEESE–PECAN FILLING

1 cup finely chopped toasted pecans
1 package (3 ounces) cream cheese, softened
1 can (8¼ ounces) crushed pineapple, well drained
2 drops yellow food color, if desired

Mix all ingredients.

CHICKEN-BACON FILLING

6 slices bacon, crisply fried and crumbled
1 cup finely chopped cooked chicken
¼ cup mayonnaise or salad dressing
2 tablespoons finely chopped green onions
   (with tops)
1 tablespoon finely snipped parsley
¼ teaspoon salt

Mix all ingredients.

Watercress Triangles

ABOUT 80 TRIANGLES

40 slices white or whole wheat sandwich
   bread
2 tablespoons dairy sour cream
½ teaspoon salt
⅛ teaspoon white pepper
4 packages (3 ounces each) cream cheese,
   softened
2 cups snipped watercress

Trim crusts from bread. Mix sour cream, salt, pepper and cream cheese. Spread cheese mixture on 20 bread slices; sprinkle with watercress. Top with remaining bread slices. Cut sandwiches diagonally into 4 triangles. Cover with dampened towel; wrap with plastic wrap. Refrigerate no longer than 24 hours.

Cucumber Sandwiches

15 SANDWICHES

10 slices sandwich bread
⅓ cup whipped cream cheese or 3
   tablespoons margarine or butter,
   softened
15 thin cucumber slices

Cut each bread slice into 3 circles. Spread each with about 1 teaspoon whipped cream cheese or ¼ teaspoon margarine. Place 1 cucumber slice between each 2 bread circles.

CUCUMBER-SHRIMP SANDWICHES: Top each cucumber slice with small amount of whipped cream cheese and cooked small shrimp.

Ribbon Sandwiches

1 loaf white sandwich bread, unsliced
1 loaf whole wheat sandwich bread,
   unsliced
Spread or fillings (below)

Trim crusts from both breads. Cut each loaf horizontally into 6 slices. For each ribbon loaf, spread 2 slices white and 1 slice whole wheat bread with ½ cup of one of the Spreads. Assemble loaf, alternating white and whole wheat slices; top with an unspread whole wheat slice. Wrap and chill. Cut loaves into slices, about ½ inch thick. Cut each slice in half.

DEVILED HAM SPREAD

1 can (4¼ ounces) deviled ham
¼ cup dairy sour cream
2 tablespoons sweet pickle relish, drained
1 tablespoon grated onion
Dash of red pepper sauce

Mix all ingredients.

CHICKEN SALAD FILLING

1 cup chopped cooked chicken
½ cup chopped celery
1½ teaspoons lemon juice
¼ teaspoon salt
⅛ teaspoon pepper
¼ cup mayonnaise or salad dressing
1 hard-cooked egg, chopped

Mix all ingredients.

HAM SALAD FILLING

2 cups ground or minced cooked ham
½ cup mayonnaise or salad dressing
½ cup chopped celery
2 tablespoons sweet pickle relish, drained
1 tablespoon chopped onion
¼ teaspoon pepper
Salt, if desired

Mix all ingredients.

Finger Sandwiches

Smoked Fish Spread (below)
Olive-Nut Spread (below)
12 slices day-old sandwich bread
Margarine or butter, softened
Sliced almonds
Fresh dill weed or parsley
Sliced pimiento-stuffed olives or pimiento

Prepare Smoked Fish Spread and Olive-Nut Spread. Trim crusts from bread slices; spread with margarine. Spread half of the bread slices with Smoked Fish Spread and remaining bread slices with Olive-Nut Spread. Cut each slice into 3 pieces. Garnish fish sandwiches with almonds and dill. Garnish olive-nut sandwiches with olive slice.

Arrange sandwiches on serving tray or plate. Cover with dampened towel; wrap with plastic wrap. Refrigerate no longer than 24 hours.

SMOKED FISH SPREAD

4 ounces smoked fish, finely chopped
2 tablespoons finely chopped celery
2 teaspoons lemon juice
Dash of pepper
1/4 cup mayonnaise or salad dressing
1 tablespoon finely chopped onion

Mix all ingredients.

OLIVE-NUT SPREAD

1 package (3 ounces) cream cheese,
*   softened*
1/2 cup finely chopped nuts
1/4 cup finely chopped pimiento-stuffed
*   olives*
2 tablespoons milk

Mix all ingredients.

Scandinavian Canapés

12 slices day-old white sandwich bread
1/4 cup margarine or butter, softened
1/2 teaspoon fresh or 1/8 teaspoon dried
   dill weed
6 thin slices fully cooked smoked ham
6 thin slices cooked turkey
1 can (11 ounces) mandarin orange
   segments, drained
1 cup seedless grape halves
1 kiwifruit, pared, thinly sliced and cut
   into fourths

Trim crusts from bread slices. Mix margarine and dill weed; spread over bread slices. Arrange ham or turkey slice on each bread slice; cut into desired shapes (a knife or small cookie cutter can be used). Top each with pieces of fruit. Garnish with watercress, mint or lettuce if desired. Arrange canapés on trays. Cover with dampened towel; wrap with plastic wrap. Refrigerate no longer than 24 hours.

Caviar Canapés

20 slices white sandwich bread
1/3 cup margarine or butter, softened
2 green onions, finely chopped
2 jars (2 ounces each) black or red caviar

Cut 4 circles from each bread slice with 1½-inch round cutter. Place rounds on ungreased cookie sheet. Set oven control to broil and/or 550°. Broil bread rounds with tops 3 to 4 inches from heat until golden brown, about 1 minute; cool. Cover and store at room temperature no longer than 24 hours.

Mix margarine and onions; spread over toasted rounds. Top with caviar. Cover and refrigerate until serving time.

Crabmeat Canapés

8 slices sandwich bread
2 cans (6 ounces each) crabmeat, drained
  and cartilage removed
¼ cup mayonnaise or salad dressing
1 teaspoon Worcestershire sauce
¼ teaspoon lemon juice
Dash red pepper sauce
Tartar sauce
Shredded process American cheese

Set oven control to broil and/or 550°. Toast bread on both sides under broiler. Remove crusts from toast. Mix crabmeat, mayonnaise, Worcestershire sauce, lemon juice and red pepper sauce. Spread each slice toast with tartar sauce; top with about ⅓ cup crabmeat mixture. Sprinkle with cheese. Broil 3 inches from heat about 3 minutes or until mixture is bubbly and lightly browned. Cut each slice into quarters.

Note: Small crisp crackers may be substituted for the toast.

Toasted Onion Canapés

¾ cup chopped onion
½ cup mayonnaise or salad dressing
¼ cup grated Parmesan cheese
20 two-inch table water crackers

Set oven control to broil and/or 550°. Mix all ingredients except crackers; spread on crackers. Broil canapés with tops 3 inches from heat, until golden brown, 2 to 3 minutes.

Open-Face Reuben Sandwiches

14 slices dark rye bread, toasted
Prepared mustard
1 can (16 ounces) sauerkraut, drained
    and chopped
5 ounces (2 2.5-ounce packages) sliced
    corned beef, finely chopped
2 cups shredded Swiss cheese (8 ounces)
½ cup mayonnaise or salad dressing

Heat oven to 375°. Spread toast lightly with mustard; place on ungreased cookie sheet. Mix sauerkraut, corned beef, cheese and mayonnaise. Spread about ⅓ cup sauerkraut mixture on each toast slice. Bake about 10 minutes or until sauerkraut mixture is hot and cheese is melted. Cut sandwiches into halves.

Avocado Toast

½ cup margarine or butter, softened
½ cup mashed avocado
2 teaspoons lime juice
1½ teaspoons snipped fresh oregano leaves
    or ½ teaspoon dried oregano leaves
1 clove garlic, finely chopped
12 slices French bread, cut diagonally
    ½ inch thick

Beat all ingredients except bread on medium speed until smooth. Set oven control to broil. Place bread on ungreased cookie sheet. Broil with tops about 4 inches from heat until light brown, 2 to 3 minutes.

Spread each slice bread generously with avocado mixture. Broil until bubbly, about 2 minutes.

Chicken-filled Puffs

Mini Puffs (below)
2 cups finely chopped cooked chicken or
    3 cans (6¾ ounces each) chicken,
    drained
⅓ cup mayonnaise or salad dressing
1 tablespoon finely chopped onion or
    ½ teaspoon instant minced onion
1 teaspoon ground ginger
2 teaspoons lemon juice
½ teaspoon salt
¼ teaspoon pepper
2 stalks celery, finely chopped (about
    ½ cup)

MINI PUFFS

1 cup water
½ cup margarine or butter
1 cup all-purpose flour
4 eggs

Prepare Mini Puffs. Mix remaining ingredients. Cover and refrigerate no longer than 24 hours.

Cut off tops of puffs with sharp knife; remove any filaments of soft dough. Fill each puff with rounded teaspoon chicken mixture; replace top. Refrigerate until serving time.

Heat oven to 400°. Heat water and margarine to rolling boil in 3-quart saucepan. Stir in flour. Stir vigorously over low heat until mixture forms a ball, about 1 minute; remove from heat. Beat in eggs, all at once; continue beating until smooth and glossy. Drop dough by slightly rounded teaspoonfuls onto ungreased cookie sheet. Bake until puffed, golden brown and dry, about 25 minutes. Cool on wire rack.

Following pages: Cold Cucumber Soup (page 23) and Chicken-filled Puffs

Mini Ham and Turkey Sandwiches

60 SANDWICHES

1 jar (8 ounces) Dijon mustard
2½ dozen cocktail buns (2 inches in diameter), sliced
2½ dozen rye cocktail buns (2 inches in diameter), sliced, or 5 dozen slices party cocktail rye bread
2 pounds thinly sliced fully cooked smoked ham
1 cup mayonnaise or salad dressing
¼ teaspoon ground cumin
2 pounds thinly sliced cooked turkey

Spread mustard over half of the buns; fill with ham. Cover with dampened towel; wrap with plastic wrap. Refrigerate no longer than 24 hours.

Mix mayonnaise and cumin. Spread mayonnaise mixture over remaining buns; fill with turkey. Cover with dampened towel; wrap with plastic wrap. Refrigerate no longer than 24 hours.

At serving time, arrange sandwiches on trays.

Cheesy Little Lunch Pizzas

4 SANDWICHES

4 English muffins, split and toasted
½ cup pizza sauce
Shredded Cheddar or mozzarella cheese
Sliced olives, crumbled cooked hamburger, chopped tomato or sliced pepperoni, if desired

Heat oven to 425°. Place toasted muffin halves on cookie sheet; top each with 1 tablespoon pizza sauce and about 1 tablespoon cheese. Add sliced olives, crumbled cooked hamburger, chopped tomato or sliced pepperoni, if desired. Bake 5 minutes or until cheese is melted.

TO MICROWAVE: Place toasted muffin halves on microwavable paper towel on microwavable plate. Microwave uncovered on high 30 to 45 seconds or until cheese is melted. Cool slightly before eating.

· 6 ·

COLD SANDWICHES

Hoagie Sandwiches

6 SANDWICHES

1 loaf (1 pound) French bread
Margarine or butter, softened
4 ounces sliced Swiss cheese
½ pound sliced salami
2 cups shredded lettuce
2 medium tomatoes, thinly sliced
1 medium onion, thinly sliced
½ pound thinly sliced fully cooked smoked
  ham
1 medium green pepper, thinly sliced
¼ cup creamy Italian salad dressing
6 long wooden picks or small skewers

Cut bread horizontally into halves. Spread bottom half with margarine. Layer cheese, salami, lettuce, tomatoes, onion, ham and green pepper on top. Drizzle with dressing; top with remaining half of bread. Secure loaf with picks; cut into 6 pieces.

Deli Sandwiches

8 frankfurter buns, split
Prepared mustard
1 pound thinly sliced cooked turkey breast
2 large dill pickles, cut lengthwise into
    fourths
1/2 pound thinly sliced fully cooked smoked
    ham
1/2 pound sliced Thuringer or salami
1 pint cream-style coleslaw

Spread each bun half with mustard. Layer turkey, pickle, ham and Thuringer on bottom half of each bun. Spoon about 1/4 cup coleslaw onto each. Top with remaining bun half.

Heidelberg Sandwiches

6 slices rye bread, toasted
Margarine or butter, softened
Lettuce leaves
3 medium tomatoes, sliced
1 1/2 pounds Braunschweiger, sliced
1 small onion, thinly sliced
1/2 cup mayonnaise or salad dressing
1/3 cup chili sauce
2 tablespoons pickle relish

Spread toast with margarine. Arrange lettuce leaves on toast. Top with tomatoes, Braunschweiger and onion. Mix mayonnaise, chili sauce and relish; spoon about 2 tablespoons over top of each.

Note: One cup bottled Thousand Island salad dressing can be substituted for the mayonnaise, chili sauce and relish.

Ham-Pineapple Sandwiches

8 slices whole wheat bread, toasted
Mayonnaise or salad dressing
1 can (8 1/4 ounces) crushed pineapple,
    drained
4 slices fully cooked smoked ham or 1 can
    (6 3/4 ounces) chunk ham
Lettuce leaves

Spread toast with mayonnaise. Spread pineapple on 4 slices toast; top with ham and lettuce. Top with remaining slices toast.

TUNA-PINEAPPLE SANDWICHES: Substitute 1 can (6 1/2 ounces) tuna, drained, for the ham. Sprinkle about 1 tablespoon thinly sliced green onion on tuna.

Muffuletta

Olive Salad (below)
1 unsliced large round or oval loaf Italian
    or sourdough bread (8- to 10-inches in
    diameter)
1/2 pound thinly sliced Italian salami
1/3 pound thinly sliced provolone cheese
1/4 pound thinly sliced fully cooked smoked
    ham

Prepare Olive Salad. Cut bread horizontally into halves. Remove 1/2-inch layer of soft bread from inside of each half to within 1/2 inch of edge. Drain Olive Salad, reserving marinade. Brush reserved marinade over cut sides of bread. Layer salami, half of the Olive Salad, the cheese, ham and remaining Olive Salad on bottom half of bread. Cover with top half of bread.

OLIVE SALAD

1 anchovy fillet, mashed
1 large clove garlic, crushed
1/3 cup olive oil
1/2 cup chopped pimiento-stuffed olives
1/2 cup chopped Greek or ripe olives
1/2 cup chopped pickled vegetables
2 tablespoons snipped parsley
1/2 teaspoon dried oregano leaves, crushed
1/8 teaspoon pepper

Stir anchovy and garlic into oil in 1-quart glass or plastic bowl until well blended. Stir in remaining ingredients. Cover and marinate in refrigerator at least 8 hours, stirring occasionally.

Beef Salad Sandwiches

1 1/2 cups chopped cooked beef
1/2 cup mayonnaise or salad dressing
1 medium stalk celery, chopped (about
    1/2 cup)
1 small onion, chopped (about 1/4 cup)
1/2 teaspoon salt
1/4 teaspoon pepper
4 whole wheat English muffins, split
Prepared mustard
Lettuce leaves

Mix all ingredients except English muffins, mustard and lettuce. Spread mustard on bottom halves of English muffins; top with lettuce. Spoon beef mixture on lettuce; top with remaining halves.

Club Waldorf Sandwich Loaf

8 SANDWICHES

1-pound loaf unsliced oval Vienna or sourdough bread
Lettuce leaves
1 small onion, thinly sliced
¼ pound thinly sliced fully cooked smoked ham
¼ pound thinly sliced cooked turkey or chicken
4 ounces sliced provolone cheese
¼ cup lemon yogurt
¼ teaspoon curry powder
1 medium apple, chopped
1 stalk celery, chopped

Cut bread into sixteen ½-inch slices, not cutting completely through to bottom of loaf. Line every other slice with lettuce, onion, ham, turkey and cheese.

Mix remaining ingredients; spoon onto cheese. To serve, cut loaf between unfilled slices into sandwiches.

BEEF WALDORF SANDWICH LOAF: Substitute ½ pound thinly sliced roast beef for the ham and turkey. Substitute ¾ teaspoon fresh dill or ¼ teaspoon dried dill weed for the curry powder.

Chicken Salad Bagel Sandwiches

4 SANDWICHES

1½ cups chopped cooked chicken or turkey
½ cup mayonnaise or salad dressing
1 medium stalk celery, chopped (about ½ cup)
1 small onion, chopped (about ¼ cup)
½ teaspoon salt
¼ teaspoon pepper
4 bagels, split
Lettuce leaves
1 medium tomato, sliced

Mix all ingredients except bagels, lettuce and tomato slices. Place lettuce and tomatoes on bottom halves of bagels. Spoon chicken mixture on tomatoes; top with remaining halves.

Ham Salad and Cheese Sandwiches

1½ cups chopped fully cooked smoked
  ham
½ cup mayonnaise or salad dressing
1 medium stalk celery, chopped (about
  ½ cup)
1 small onion, chopped (about ¼ cup)
1 teaspoon prepared mustard
4 ounces Cheddar cheese, sliced
8 slices multigrain bread

Mix all ingredients except cheese and bread. Place cheese on 4 slices bread. Spoon ham mixture on cheese; top with remaining bread.

Tuna Cobb Salad Sandwiches

1 can (6½ ounces) tuna, drained
4 to 6 slices bacon, crisply cooked and
  crumbled
2 hard-cooked eggs, chopped
1 avocado, peeled and cut into cubes
¼ to ⅓ cup blue cheese dressing
Shredded iceberg or romaine lettuce
2 medium tomatoes, thinly sliced
4 croissants, split

Mix tuna, bacon, eggs, avocado and dressing. Place lettuce and tomatoes on bottom halves of croissants. Spoon tuna mixture on tomatoes; top with remaining halves.

Following pages: Chilled Yogurt-Vegetable Soup (page 24) and Chicken Salad Bagel Sandwiches

Tunawiches

½ loaf (1-pound size) French bread
Spicy brown mustard
½ cup mayonnaise or salad dressing
2 cans (6½ ounces each) tuna, drained
1 cup shredded Muenster cheese
   (4 ounces)
Salad greens
1 medium cucumber, thinly sliced
1 medium tomato, cut into 6 slices

Cut loaf of bread lengthwise into halves; spread mustard over cut sides. Mix mayonnaise and tuna; spread on mustard.

Top with cheese, salad greens, cucumber and tomato. Cut each bread half into thirds. Spoon dollop of mayonnaise onto each sandwich, if desired.

Tuna Salad–Avocado Sandwiches

1 9¼-ounce can tuna in water, drained
1 large stalk celery, chopped (about
   ⅓ cup)
2 tablespoons sweet pickle relish
½ cup mayonnaise or salad dressing
Salt and pepper to taste
12 slices whole wheat or white bread,
   toasted
1 avocado, thinly sliced

Mix all ingredients except toast and avocado slices. Spread tuna mixture on one side of 6 slices toast. Arrange avocado slices on tuna mixture; top with remaining toast.

Shrimp and Avocado Club Sandwiches

4 SANDWICHES

Mayonnaise or salad dressing
12 slices white bread, toasted
4 lettuce leaves
12 slice tomatoes (about 2 medium)
12 slices bacon, crisply cooked
2 cans (4¼ ounces each) large shrimp,
    rinsed and drained
1 large avocado, peeled and thinly sliced

Spread mayonnaise over one side of each slice toast. Place lettuce leaf, 3 slices tomato and 3 slices bacon on each of 4 slices toast. Top with another slice toast.

Arrange shrimp on top; arrange avocado slices on shrimp. Top with third slice toast; secure with wooden picks. Cut sandwiches diagonally into 4 triangles.

TURKEY AND AVOCADO CLUB SANDWICHES: Substitute 4 slices cooked turkey or chicken for the shrimp.

Curried Egg and Shrimp Sandwiches

6 SANDWICHES

1 package (8 ounces) cream cheese,
    softened
¼ cup dairy sour cream
1 teaspoon curry powder
¼ teaspoon salt
6 slices multigrain bread, toasted
3 hard-cooked eggs, sliced
1 can (4¼ ounces) tiny shrimp, drained
¼ cup finely chopped green onions (with
    tops)

Mix cream cheese, sour cream, curry powder and salt; spread over toast. Arrange egg slices on cream cheese mixture. Top with shrimp and onions.

Egg Salad Sandwiches

6 hard-cooked eggs, chopped
1/2 cup mayonnaise or salad dressing
1 medium stalk celery, chopped (about
   1/2 cup)
1 small onion, chopped (about 1/4 cup)
1/2 teaspoon salt
1/4 teaspoon pepper
8 slices sourdough bread, toasted
Alfalfa sprouts
1 medium tomato, sliced

Mix all ingredients except toast, sprouts and tomatoes. Place sprouts and tomato slices on 4 slices toast. Spoon egg mixture on tomatoes; top with remaining slices toast.

Peanut Butter and Apples on Raisin Bread

3/4 cup chunky peanut butter
1/4 cup apricot preserves
1 teaspoon dry mustard
8 slices raisin bread
2 medium pared or unpared eating
   apples, thinly sliced
Salad greens

Mix peanut butter, preserves and mustard; spread over one side of 4 slices bread. Arrange apple slices and salad greens on peanut butter mixture. Top with remaining bread.

Peanut Butter BLT Sandwiches

4 SANDWICHES

Peanut butter
8 slices white bread, toasted
2 medium tomatoes, sliced
Lettuce leaves
8 slices bacon, crisply cooked

Spread peanut butter over one side of 4 slices toast. Arrange tomato slices, lettuce leaves and bacon on peanut butter. Top with remaining toast.

Brie and Cucumber on Rye

4 SANDWICHES

1/2 English cucumber or 1 small cucumber
8 ounces Brie cheese, cut into 1/4-inch pieces
1/4 cup finely chopped green onions (with tops)
1/4 cup oil-and-vinegar dressing
3/4 teaspoon snipped fresh or 1/4 teaspoon dried dill weed
Margarine or butter
4 slices rye bread
Salad greens

Cut cucumber lengthwise into halves; cut each half into thin slices. Toss cucumber, cheese, onions, dressing and dill weed.

Spread margarine over one side of each slice bread; top with salad greens. Spoon cheese mixture onto greens. Garnish each sandwich with 1 cooked shrimp and fresh dill weed if desired.

ZUCCHINI AND CREAM CHEESE ON RYE: Substitute 1 medium zucchini for the English cucumber and 1 package (8 ounces) cream cheese for the Brie cheese.

Following pages: Dried Fruit Soup (page 22) and Brie and Cucumber on Rye

Swiss Cheese and Vegetables in Pita Breads

6 SANDWICHES

1 cup shredded Swiss cheese (4 ounces)
1/2 cup thinly sliced cauliflowerets
1/4 cup mayonnaise or salad dressing
1 teaspoon snipped fresh or 1/2 teaspoon
  dried dill weed
1/2 teaspoon salt
1 medium tomato, chopped
1 small zucchini or carrot, shredded
3 pita breads (6 inches in diameter), cut
  into halves
Salad greens

Mix all ingredients except pita breads and salad greens. Separate pita breads along cut sides to form pockets. Arrange salad greens and vegetable mixture in pockets.

Crunchy Cottage Cheese Sandwiches

6 SANDWICHES

1 container (12 ounces) small curd
  creamed cottage cheese
1/2 green pepper, finely chopped, or 1/2 cup
  chopped celery
1 dill pickle, finely chopped
1 tablespoon fresh snipped or
  freeze-dried chives
12 slices multigrain bread, toasted
Lettuce leaves

Mix cottage cheese, green pepper, dill pickle and chives. Spread cottage cheese mixture on one side of 6 slices toast. Top with lettuce leaves and remaining toast.

· 7 ·

HOT SANDWICHES

Hot Club Sandwiches

8 hard rolls
Margarine or butter, softened
1 pound sliced fully cooked smoked ham
½ pound sliced cooked turkey or chicken
1 cup shredded mozzarella cheese (about
    4 ounces)
½ cup crumbled blue cheese

Heat oven to 425°. Cut rolls horizontally into thirds. Spread each cut surface with margarine. Place ham on bottom sections of rolls; add second sections of rolls. Top with turkey. Mix cheeses; spread over turkey. Top with third sections of rolls. Wrap each sandwich in aluminum foil. Heat wrapped sandwiches on oven rack until hot, 15 to 20 minutes.

Philly Beef Sandwiches

2 medium onions, sliced
2 tablespoons margarine or butter
6 hoagie or frankfurter buns, split and
    toasted
1¼ pounds thinly sliced roast beef
12 slices process American cheese

Cook and stir onions in margarine until tender, about 10 minutes. Set oven control to broil. Place bottom halves of buns on ungreased cookie sheet; top with onions and beef. Cut cheese slices into halves; place 4 halves on each sandwich. Broil with tops 5 to 6 inches from heat just until cheese is melted, 2 to 3 minutes. Top each with remaining bun half.

Barbecued Roast Beef Sandwiches

6 SANDWICHES

Zesty Barbecue Sauce (below)
1 pound thinly sliced roast beef, cut
* into 1-inch strips (about 3 cups)*
6 hamburger buns, split

ZESTY BARBECUE SAUCE

½ cup catsup
¼ cup vinegar
2 tablespoons chopped onion
1 tablespoon Worcestershire sauce
2 teaspoons packed brown sugar
¼ teaspoon dry mustard
1 clove garlic, crushed

Prepare Zesty Barbecue Sauce. Stir beef into sauce. Cover and simmer until beef is heated through, about 5 minutes. Fill each hamburger bun with beef mixture.

Heat all ingredients to boiling in 1-quart saucepan over medium heat, stirring constantly; reduce heat. Simmer uncovered 15 minutes, stirring sauce occasionally.

QUICK BARBECUED ROAST BEEF SANDWICHES: Substitute 1 cup barbecue sauce for the Zesty Barbecue Sauce and 3 packages (3 ounces each) smoked sliced chicken, ham, turkey, beef or pastrami, cut into 1-inch strips, for the beef.

TO MICROWAVE: Mix sauce ingredients in 4-cup microwavable measure. Microwave uncovered on high 2 minutes; stir. Microwave uncovered until sauce is slightly thickened, 2 to 4 minutes longer. Stir beef into sauce. Cover tightly and microwave until beef is hot, 5 to 7 minutes.

Barbecued Pork Sandwiches

4 pounds fresh pork boneless blade,
  Boston or arm picnic roast
Salt and pepper
1/4 cup packed brown sugar
1/4 cup vinegar
1/4 cup molasses
2 tablespoons dry mustard
1 tablespoon Worcestershire sauce
1/2 teaspoon salt
1/4 teaspoon liquid smoke
1/4 teaspoon red pepper sauce
2 cloves garlic, crushed
1 bottle (12 ounces) chili sauce
1 can (8 ounces) tomato sauce
10 hamburger buns

Place pork, fat side up, on rack in shallow roasting pan; sprinkle with salt and pepper. Insert meat thermometer so tip is in center of thickest part of pork and does not rest in fat.

Roast uncovered in 325° oven until thermometer registers 170°, about 2½ hours. Cool; shred into pieces with 2 forks. Heat remaining ingredients except hamburger buns to boiling in 3-quart saucepan. Cook, stirring occasionally, until thickened, about 20 minutes. Stir in shredded pork. Cover and refrigerate no longer than 24 hours.

Heat pork mixture to boiling over medium heat, stirring occasionally; reduce heat. Simmer uncovered until hot, about 15 minutes. Serve pork mixture with buns.

Toasty Hot Dog Roll-ups

8 slices sandwich bread
1/2 cup margarine or butter, melted
Prepared mustard
4 slices process American cheese, cut
  diagonally into triangles
8 frankfurters

Heat oven to 375°. Brush one side of bread with half of the margarine; spread with mustard. Place cheese triangle on mustard; top with frankfurter. Bring sides of bread up over frankfurter; secure with wooden picks. Brush outsides of the roll-ups with remaining margarine. Place on ungreased cookie sheet. Bake until golden brown, 10 to 15 minutes.

Hot Antipasto Poor Boys

1/4 cup creamy Italian dressing
2 tablespoons grated Parmesan cheese
1 cup cherry tomatoes, cut into fourths
1 can (14 ounces) artichoke hearts,
    drained and cut into fourths
1 package (5 ounces) pepperoni, cut up
1 can (2 1/4 ounces) sliced ripe olives,
    drained
2 poor boy buns, split*
1/2 cup shredded mozzarella cheese
    (2 ounces)

Mix dressing and Parmesan cheese in large bowl; toss with tomatoes, artichoke hearts, pepperoni and olives. Set oven control to broil. Place buns, cut sides up, on ungreased cookie sheet. Broil with tops about 6 inches from heat until golden brown, about 5 minutes.

Spoon pepperoni mixture onto buns. Sprinkle about 2 tablespoons mozzarella cheese over each. Broil until cheese is hot and bubbly, 3 to 4 minutes.

*4 frankfurter buns, split, can be substituted for the poor boy buns. Sprinkle 1 tablespoon mozzarella cheese over pepperoni mixture on each bun.

Chicken and Artichoke Croissants

4 croissants, split lengthwise into halves
1 cup sliced mushrooms (about 3 ounces)
3 tablespoons margarine or butter
1 tablespoon all-purpose flour
1/2 teaspoon garlic salt
1/2 cup milk
1/4 cup dry white wine
1 cup cut-up cooked chicken or turkey
1/2 cup shredded Swiss cheese (2 ounces)
1 jar (6 ounces) marinated artichoke
    hearts, drained and cut into halves

Heat croissants in 300° oven until hot, about 10 minutes. Cook and stir mushrooms in 2 tablespoons of the margarine in 1 1/2-quart saucepan over medium heat until tender, 2 to 3 minutes. Remove mushrooms; reserve.

Heat remaining 1 tablespoon margarine in same saucepan until melted; stir in flour and garlic salt. Cook, stirring constantly, until bubbly. Remove from heat; stir in milk and wine. Heat to boiling, stirring constantly. Boil and stir 1 minute.

Stir in mushrooms and remaining ingredients; heat until hot. Spoon over croissant bottoms; add tops.

Chicken Tacos

10 TACOS

2 cups cut-up cooked chicken
3/4 teaspoon salt
1 can (4 ounces) chopped green chilies,
    drained
1 small onion, sliced
2 tablespoons vegetable oil
10 taco shells
1 small avocado
Lemon juice
1/2 teaspoon salt
1 cup shredded Monterey Jack or
    Cheddar cheese (about 4 ounces)
2 cups shredded lettuce
1/3 cup sliced pimiento-stuffed olives
Taco sauce
Dairy sour cream

Heat chicken, 3/4 teaspoon salt, the chilies and onion in oil in 10-inch skillet over medium heat, stirring occasionally, until chicken is hot. Heat taco shells as directed on package. Cut avocado lengthwise into slices; sprinkle with lemon juice and 1/2 teaspoon salt.

Spoon about 1/4 cup chicken mixture into each shell. Top with cheese, lettuce, olives and avocado. Serve with taco sauce and sour cream.

Broiled Cheese Sandwiches

8 SANDWICHES

1 cup shredded Cheddar cheese (about
    4 ounces)
1 cup shredded Monterey Jack cheese
    (about 4 ounces)
1 medium onion, chopped (about 1/2 cup)
1/3 cup margarine or butter, softened
8 slices diagonally cut French bread
    (about 3/4 inch thick), toasted

Mix Cheddar and Monterey Jack cheeses, onion and margarine. Spread to edges of toast. Set oven control to broil and/or 550°. Broil with tops about 5 inches from heat until cheese is melted and bubbly, about 2 minutes.

BROILED WINE-CHEESE SANDWICHES: Place toast in ungreased 15 1/2 × 10 1/2 × 1-inch jelly roll pan. Drizzle 1 tablespoon dry white wine over each slice toast; spread with cheese mixture. Continue as directed.

Following pages: Guacamole Soup (page 25) and Chicken Tacos

Gyros

1 pound ground lamb or beef
2 tablespoons water
1 tablespoon lemon juice
1 teaspoon salt
1/2 teaspoon ground cumin
1/2 teaspoon dried oregano leaves
1/4 teaspoon pepper
2 cloves garlic, crushed
1 small onion, chopped (about 1/4 cup)
2 tablespoons vegetable oil
4 pita breads (6 inches in diameter)
2 cups shredded lettuce
1/2 cup plain yogurt
1 tablespoon snipped fresh or 1 teaspoon
    dried mint leaves
1 teaspoon sugar
1 small cucumber, seeded and chopped
    (about 3/4 cup)
1 medium tomato, chopped

Mix lamb, water, lemon juice, salt, cumin, oregano, pepper, garlic and onion. Shape into 4 thin patties. Cook patties in oil over medium heat, turning frequently, until done, 10 to 12 minutes.

Split each bread halfway around edge with knife; separate to form pocket. Place patty in each pocket; top with lettuce. Mix yogurt, snipped mint and sugar; stir in cucumber. Spoon onto lettuce; top with tomato.

Grilled Port-Cheese Sandwiches

1 package (8 ounces) cream cheese,
    softened
1/4 cup ruby port or sweet red wine
2 cups shredded Cheddar cheese
    (8 ounces)
20 slices French bread, each 1/2 inch thick
Margarine or butter, softened

Mix cream cheese and wine, using spoon, until well blended. Stir in Cheddar cheese. For each sandwich, spread about 3 tablespoons of the cheese mixture evenly on 1 slice bread. Top with second slice. Spread top slices of bread with margarine.

Place 5 sandwiches, margarine sides down, in 10-inch skillet. Spread top slices of bread with margarine. Cook uncovered over medium heat until golden brown, 3 to 4 minutes; turn. Cook until golden brown and cheese is warm, about 2 minutes longer. Repeat with remaining sandwiches. Serve with fresh fruit, if desired.

Mozzarella and Tomato Melts

4 SANDWICHES

4 slices Italian bread, each 1 inch thick
8 ounces mozzarella cheese, sliced
2 medium tomatoes, thinly sliced
Salt and freshly ground pepper
½ cup Pesto (below) or prepared pesto

Set oven control to broil. Place bread on ungreased cookie sheet. Broil with tops about 4 inches from heat until golden brown; turn. Divide cheese among bread slices. Broil just until cheese begins to melt.

Arrange tomatoes on cheese; sprinkle with salt and pepper. Top with Pesto. Garnish with fresh basil leaves, if desired.

PESTO

2 cups firmly packed snipped fresh basil
*   leaves*
¾ cup grated Parmesan cheese
¾ cup olive oil
2 tablespoons pine nuts
4 cloves garlic

Place all ingredients in blender. Cover and blend on medium speed, stopping blender occasionally to scrape sides, until smooth, about 3 minutes.

Note: Freeze any remaining Pesto up to 6 months. Let stand at room temperature until thawed, at least 4 hours.

Broiled Seafood Sandwiches

4 SANDWICHES

1 cup mixed bite-size pieces cooked
*   crabmeat, lobster or shrimp**
1 cup shredded Swiss cheese (4 ounces)
½ cup mayonnaise or salad dressing
1 green onion (with top), thinly sliced
4 slices whole grain bread, toasted
Alfalfa sprouts

Mix all ingredients except toast and sprouts. Set oven control to broil. Arrange sprouts on toast; top with seafood mixture.

Place sandwiches on ungreased cookie sheet. Broil with tops about 4 inches from heat until seafood mixture is hot and bubbly, about 2 minutes.

*1 cup bite-size pieces cooked fish (salmon, cod, halibut, tuna, swordfish) can be substituted for the crabmeat, lobster or shrimp.

Following pages: Easy Spinach Soup (page 18) and Broiled Seafood Sandwiches

Broiled Bean Sandwiches

12 SANDWICHES

6 French rolls
1 can (16 ounces) refried beans
¾ cup shredded Cheddar cheese (about
3 ounces)

Cut rolls lengthwise into halves. Set oven control to broil and/or 550°. Broil halves until golden brown. Spread each half with 2 tablespoons refried beans. Sprinkle each with 1 tablespoon cheese. Broil with tops 2 to 3 inches from heat until cheese is melted, about 1½ minutes.

Hot Vegetable Sandwiches

6 SANDWICHES

6 unsliced whole wheat or white
hamburger buns
1½ cups shredded Swiss cheese (about
6 ounces)
¼ cup mayonnaise or salad dressing
½ teaspoon salt
1½ teaspoons fresh or ½ teaspoon dried
basil leaves
2 small zucchini, thinly sliced (about
1 cup)
1 large tomato, chopped (about 1 cup)
1 medium onion, chopped (about ½ cup)
1 can (2 ounces) sliced ripe olives,
drained

Heat oven to 350°. Cut thin slice from top of each bun; reserve. Remove center from each bun, leaving ¼-inch wall. (Use removed bread for bread crumbs or stuffing.) Mix cheese, mayonnaise, salt and basil; spread about ¼ cup in bottom of each bun. Mix zucchini, tomato, onion and olives; divide among buns. Top with reserved tops of buns. Wrap each sandwich in heavy-duty aluminum foil. Heat on oven rack until hot and cheese is melted, about 25 minutes.

Denver Pocket Sandwiches

1 medium onion, chopped (about ½ cup)
1 small green pepper, chopped (about
   ½ cup)
2 tablespoons margarine or butter
6 eggs
½ cup chopped fully cooked smoked ham
   or 1 can (6¾ ounces) chunk ham
1 jar (2 ounces) diced pimiento, drained
¼ teaspoon salt
⅛ teaspoon pepper
6 large pita breads

Cook and stir onion and green pepper in margarine in 10-inch skillet over medium heat until onion is tender. Beat eggs slightly; stir in ham, pimiento, salt and pepper. Pour egg mixture into skillet. Cook over low heat, gently lifting cooking portions with spatula so that thin uncooked portion can flow to bottom. Avoid constant stirring. Cook until eggs are thickened throughout but still moist, 3 to 5 minutes. Divide among pita breads.

Puff Sandwich Loaf

2½ cups variety baking mix
1½ cups mayonnaise or salad dressing
½ teaspoon salt
2 eggs
4 cups shredded Swiss cheese (16 ounces)
2 avocados, chopped
1 medium zucchini, chopped
1 loaf (1 pound) French bread
1 cup alfalfa sprouts

Mix baking mix, mayonnaise, salt and eggs. Stir in cheese, avocados and zucchini. Cut bread crosswise into halves; cut each half lengthwise into halves. Divide cheese mixture among bread pieces, spreading evenly to edges.

Heat oven to 450°. Bake on ungreased cookie sheet until puffy and golden brown, about 12 minutes. Cut each piece diagonally into slices, keeping slices together to retain shape of bread. Sprinkle with alfalfa sprouts.

Following pages: Hot Vegetable Sandwiches and Quick Creamy Potato Soup (page 52)

Grilled Peanut Butter and Banana

Peanut butter
8 slices English muffin bread
2 medium bananas
Margarine or butter, softened

Spread peanut butter over one side of 4 slices bread; slice bananas and arrange on top. Top with remaining bread; spread top slices with margarine.

Place sandwiches, margarine sides down, in skillet. Spread top slices with margarine. Cook uncovered over medium heat until bottoms are golden brown, about 4 minutes; turn. Cook until bottoms are golden brown and peanut butter is melted, 2 to 3 minutes longer.

GRILLED PEANUT BUTTER AND BANANA WITH BA-CON: Place cooked bacon slices on bananas before topping with remaining bread.

RED SPOON TIPS

Soups on the Run

Follow these tips to make meals away from home delicious and safe. Remember, food that has been kept too long at room temperature can be a safety hazard, so always refrigerate your lunch until it's time to eat.

▪ Cook up a big pot of soup on the weekend and bring a serving of it for lunch during the week. Soup can be kept in the refrigerator for 2 to 3 days.

▪ Put soup in a leakproof and microwavable container and refrigerate until serving time. Microwave it to reheat. Brothlike soups reheat especially well in the microwave because they heat quickly and evenly without separating.

Sandwiches on the Run

Sandwiches are classic children's lunchbox fare, but they can be very practical for adults, too. You can choose your favorite fillings—and use just as much or as little as you like; you can use up leftovers, and your homemade sandwich will almost certainly be a savings over a restaurant or take-out lunch. Like soup, sandwiches are easy to make ahead of time. Make a nice variety of sandwiches once a week.

▪ Wrap the prepared sandwiches in plastic wrap, label them and put them in the freezer. Each day you can pick out a premade sandwich! Your sandwich will thaw in the refrigerator by lunchtime. Do not refreeze thawed sandwiches.

▪ Leave out lettuce, tomato, celery, cucumber, mayonnaise, sour cream, cooked eggs and jelly—they don't freeze well. Pack them separately and add them to the sandwich just before eating.

▪ Take a lunch box; it will insulate better than a lunch bag.

▪ If you decide to make your sandwich the night before, you can wrap it and keep it in the refrigerator overnight. Refrigerate it when you get to the office or school.

Freezing Soup

Soup freezes exceptionally well. You can cook up a double recipe of your favorite soup and freeze half. It will save you time, and you'll have a delicious soup waiting for you in the freezer on a day when you don't have the time to make it from scratch.

- Select a plastic freezer container that holds enough soup for one meal—a quart container holds 4 to 6 servings and a pint container holds 2 to 3 servings.

- Use containers with wide openings so soup can be easily removed when only partially thawed.

- Leave ½-inch headspace in quart containers and ¼-inch headspace in pint containers because liquids expand when frozen.

- Label each container with the name of the soup, number of servings and date you froze it.

- Soups and stews keep well in the freezer for 2 to 3 months.

- Thaw frozen soups in the refrigerator.

- Be sure to use fully thawed soups immediately.

- Although some flavors intensify in the freezing process, onion gradually loses its flavor. Season to taste after reheating.

- Freezing makes potatoes grainy and soft, so leave potatoes out of the soup until it's time to reheat. Be sure to cook the potatoes before you add them to the soup.

Freezing Sandwiches

See Sandwiches on the Run (page 97) for tips on general freezing guidelines. Party sandwiches are wonderful to have on hand in your freezer, whether unexpected company turns up or you want to plan ahead for a party. See Party Sandwiches (page 53) for a delicious variety of party sandwich recipes. When you follow these tips, you'll have delicious sandwiches at your fingertips.

- Freeze the sandwiches with waxed paper between layers, using a separate container for each kind of sandwich.

- Do not freeze sandwiches with fillings of lettuce, celery, tomatoes, large amounts of mayonnaise, salad dressing, sour cream and cooked egg whites. You can add those fillings just before serving.

- Wrap and freeze uncut rolled and ribbon sandwiches.

- Freeze sandwich loaves unfrosted.

- Slice rolled or ribbon sandwiches while slightly frozen. Thaw whole sandwich loaves in wrapping in the refrigerator for 2 to 3 hours.

- Thaw small sandwiches on serving plate at room temperature 15 to 20 minutes before serving.

Flavored Butters

Flavored butter can make your sandwiches special. Try some of these easy-to-make and sure-to-please butters on your favorite sandwiches.

Lemon-Herb Butter

1/2 cup butter or margarine, softened
1 tablespoon lemon juice
1 tablespoon chopped fresh or 1 teaspoon
dried parsley flakes
1 1/2 teaspoons chopped fresh or 1/2
teaspoon dried basil leaves

Blend all ingredients. Serve on seafood and beef sandwiches.

Curry Butter

1/2 cup butter or margarine, softened
1 teaspoon curry powder

Blend butter and curry powder. Serve on lamb or ham sandwiches.

Garlic Butter

1 to 2 cloves of garlic, minced
1/2 cup butter or margarine, softened
2 teaspoons chopped fresh parsley, basil,
marjoram, or 1 teaspoon chopped
fresh oregano, if desired

Blend all ingredients. Serve on beef, chicken or turkey sandwiches.

Horseradish Butter

1/2 cup butter or margarine, softened
1 tablespoon prepared horseradish

Blend butter and horseradish. Serve on roast beef or ham sandwiches.

Dill Butter

1/2 cup butter or margarine, softened
2 teaspoons chopped fresh or 1 teaspoon
dried dill weed

Blend butter and dill weed. Serve on roast beef or ham sandwiches.

Mayonnaises

Flavored mayonnaises can add a special taste to your favorite sandwiches. These easy recipes are a fun change from your regular mayonnaise or salad dressing.

Tomato-Cucumber Mayonnaise
ABOUT 1¾ CUPS

1 cup mayonnaise or salad dressing
½ cup finely chopped tomato, drained
½ cup finely chopped and seeded
   cucumber
1 teaspoon minced onion

Mix all ingredients. Chill to blend flavors.

Chipotle Mayonnaise
ABOUT 1 CUP

½ cup mayonnaise or salad dressing
½ cup dairy sour cream
⅛ teaspoon dried oregano leaves, if
   desired
2 canned chipotle chilies in adobo sauce,
   finely chopped

Mix all ingredients. Cover and refrigerate until chilled, about 1 hour.

Homemade Broths

There's something wonderfully satisfying about making a soup completely from scratch, and broth, the base of many soups, isn't hard to make. Try these recipes in soups that call for broth.

Beef Broth and Cooked Beef

10 CUPS BROTH AND
3½ CUPS CUBED COOKED BEEF

4 pounds beef shank cross cuts
12 cups cold water
2 carrots, chopped (about 1 cup)
2 stalks celery with leaves, chopped (about 1 cup)
1 medium onion, chopped (about ½ cup)
2 teaspoons salt
¼ teaspoon dried thyme leaves
10 peppercorns
5 whole cloves
3 sprigs parsley
1 bay leaf

Remove beef from bones; cut beef into 1-inch cubes. Remove marrow from center of bones. Heat marrow in Dutch oven over low heat until melted, or heat ¼ cup vegetable oil until hot. Cook and stir beef in marrow until beef is brown. Add water and bones. Heat to boiling; skim foam. Stir in remaining ingredients. Heat to boiling; skim foam. Cover and simmer 3 hours.

Strain broth through cheesecloth-lined sieve. Discard bones, vegetables and seasonings. Skim fat from broth. Clarify broth if desired (see below). Use immediately, or cover and refrigerate broth and beef in separate containers up to 24 hours, or freeze for future use.

TO CLARIFY BROTH: Beat 1 egg white, 1 tablespoon water and 1 broken egg shell. Stir into strained broth. Heat to boiling, stirring constantly. Boil 2 minutes. Remove from heat; let stand 5 minutes. Strain through double-thickness cheesecloth.

Note: Hot clarified Beef Broth can be served as an appetizer. Garnish each ½-cup serving with 1 thin lemon slice or 3 thinly sliced mushrooms.

Chicken Broth and Cooked Chicken

3- to 3½-pound broiler-fryer chicken, cut up*
4½ cups cold water
1½ teaspoons salt
½ teaspoon pepper
1 stalk celery with leaves, chopped (about ½ cup)
1 medium carrot, sliced (about ½ cup)
1 small onion, sliced
1 sprig parsley

Remove any excess fat from chicken. Place chicken, giblets (except liver) and neck in Dutch oven. Add remaining ingredients. Heat to boiling; skim foam. Reduce heat; cover and simmer until thickest pieces of chicken are done, about 45 minutes.

Remove chicken from broth; cool chicken just until cool enough to handle, about 10 minutes. Strain broth through cheesecloth-lined sieve. Remove chicken from bones and skin in pieces as large as possible; cut up chicken. Skim fat from broth. Use immediately, or cover and refrigerate broth and chicken in separate containers up to 24 hours, or freeze for future use.

*3 to 3½ pounds chicken necks, backs and giblets can be used to make broth.

Note: To cook 4- to 6-pound stewing chicken, increase water to 7 cups and salt to 1 tablespoon. Increase simmering time to about 2½ hours. 5 to 6 cups broth and about 5 cups cut-up cooked chicken.

Fish Broth

1½ pounds fish bones and trimmings
4 cups cold water
1½ cups dry white wine
1 tablespoon lemon juice
1 teaspoon salt
½ teaspoon ground thyme
1 large celery stalk, chopped (about
  ½ cup)
1 small onion, sliced
3 mushrooms, chopped
3 sprigs parsley
1 bay leaf

Rinse fish bones and trimmings under running cold water; drain. Mix bones, trimmings and remaining ingredients in Dutch oven. Heat to boiling; skim foam. Reduce heat; cover and simmer 30 minutes. Strain through cheesecloth-lined sieve. Discard skin, bones, vegetables and seasonings. Use immediately, or cover and refrigerate up to 24 hours, or freeze for future use.

Quick Brown Stock

2 cans (10½ ounces each) condensed beef
  broth (bouillon)
1 soup can water
¼ cup sliced onions
¼ cup sliced carrots
¼ cup sliced celery
2 parsley sprigs
1 small bay leaf
⅛ teaspoon dried thyme leaves

Mix all ingredients. Heat to boiling; reduce heat. Cover and simmer 30 minutes; strain.

QUICK WHITE STOCK: Substitute 2 cans (10¾ ounces each) condensed chicken broth for the condensed beef broth.

Economy Cuts of Meat

Because most hearty soups and stews simmer for a lengthy period of time, less expensive cuts of meat can be used—and they'll be quite tender when cooked.

▪ Beef stew meat is usually cut from the boneless chuck or round sections.

▪ Pork stew meat is usually cut from the Boston shoulder or picnic shoulder sections.

▪ Lamb stew meat is usually cut from the shoulder or leg sections or from the neck.

▪ Veal stew meat is usually cut from the shoulder or leg sections.

Compare the price per pound of these cuts (including the waste) with ready-cut meat. You may find it more economical to cut up the meat yourself.

Soup Shortcuts

Of course you won't always have time to whip up your own chicken or beef broth. Canned soups and broths are certainly delicious and convenient substitutes. Here are other ways to cut down on preparation time without cutting down on flavor.

- To make broth from bouillon: For each cup of broth, simply dissolve 1 bouillon cube or 1 teaspoon instant bouillon in 1 cup of boiling water.

- Make an impromptu soup by adding leftover, cooked vegetables to broth or bouillon. Add your favorite spices and some croutons or crackers for garnish, and you have a delicious soup in no time.

- Salad bars in delis and groceries can be a boon to the chef in a hurry. If you don't have time to chop and peel vegetables for soup, you can pick up already prepared vegetables in many stores.

Soup Garnishes

Soup is delicious on its own, but garnishes can add a special flavor or texture. Try some of these garnishes on your favorite soups:

- Lemon or lime slices or zest
- Bell pepper rings
- Sliced green onions
- Thinly sliced carrots
- Croutons
- Crackers, oyster crackers, corn chips
- Popcorn
- Sprigs or snipped parsley or dill
- Paprika
- Toasted nuts
- Shredded cheese
- Hard-cooked eggs—sliced, crumbled or chopped
- Cooked, crumbled bacon
- Sour cream, whipped cream or yogurt

Canned Combinations

Canned soups can be a quick way to make a satisfying meal. Try some of these soup combinations for a new twist on your old favorites. You'll enjoy the new flavors, and may even be inspired to create your own combinations.

CONDENSED SOUP 1 CAN EACH	LIQUID	ADDITION	SERVINGS
Bean with Bacon (11 ounces) Vegetable (10½ ounces)	2 soup cans water		5 servings (1 cup each)
Cheddar Cheese (11 ounces) Split Pea with Ham and Bacon (11½ ounces)	1 soup can water 1 soup can milk		5 servings (1 cup each)
Chicken Noodle (10¾ ounces) French Onion (10½ ounces)	2 soup cans water		5 servings (1 cup each)
Cream of Chicken (10¾ ounces)	1 soup can water	¼ teaspoon curry powder	3 servings (about ¾ cup each)
Tomato (10¾ ounces)	1 soup can milk	¼ teaspoon ground cloves	3 servings (about ¾ cup each)
Tomato (10¾ ounces) Beef Noodle (10¾ ounces)	1 soup can water 1 soup can milk		5 servings (1 cup each)
Tomato (10¾ ounces) Chicken Gumbo (10¾ ounces)	1 soup can water 1 soup can milk		5 servings (1 cup each)

Home-baked Bread

There's a popular phrase: "The greatest thing since sliced bread." Although sliced bread and other "store-bought" breads are wonderfully convenient—and quite tasty, too—there's something special about fresh home-baked bread. We've included a basic recipe for a hearty white bread. Slice it for sandwiches or tear off warm, crusty pieces to eat with a hearty soup.

Traditional White Bread   2 LOAVES

6 to 7 cups all-purpose or unbleached
   flour*
3 tablespoons sugar
1 tablespoon salt
2 tablespoons shortening
*2 packages regular or quick-acting active
   dry yeast*
2¼ cups very warm water (120° to 130°)

Mix 3½ cups of the flour, the sugar, salt, shortening and yeast in 4-quart bowl; add warm water. Beat on low speed, scraping bowl frequently, 1 minute. Beat on medium speed, scraping bowl frequently, 1 minute. Stir in enough remaining flour, 1 cup at a time, to make dough easy to handle.

Turn dough onto lightly floured surface; knead until smooth and elastic, about 10 minutes. Place in greased 2½-quart bowl; turn greased side up. Cover and let rise in warm place until double, 40 to 60 minutes. (Dough is ready if indentation remains when touched.)

Punch down dough; divide into halves. Let rest 5 minutes. Flatten each half with hands or rolling pin into rectangle, 18 × 9 inches, on lightly floured surface. (If dough shrinks, gently stretch into rectangle.) Fold 9-inch sides crosswise into thirds, overlapping sides. Roll up tightly toward you, beginning at open end. Pinch edge of dough into roll to seal well. Press each end with side of hand to seal; fold ends under loaf. Place loaves, seam sides down, in 2 greased loaf pans, 9 × 5 × 3 or 8½ × 4½ × 2½ inches. Brush loaves lightly with margarine if desired. Let rise until double, 35 to 50 minutes.

Heat oven to 425°. Place loaves on low rack so that tops of pans are in center of oven. Bake until deep golden brown and loaves sound hollow when tapped, 25 to 30 minutes. Remove from pans. Brush loaves with margarine if desired; cool on wire rack.

*If using self-rising flour, omit salt.

Menus

Soups and sandwiches are perfect for both casual and formal entertaining, and these menus will give you ideas for delicious meals.

HEARTY WINTER DINNER

Smoky Bean Soup (page 28)

Barbecued Pork Sandwiches (page 83)

Green salad

Apple pie a la mode

Hot chocolate

SUMMER AFTERNOON TEA

Fresh Fruit Soup (page 19)

Watercress Triangles (page 57)

Cucumber Sandwiches (page 57)

Sugar cookies

Minted iced tea

SPRING LUNCH

Cut-up fresh fruit

Cold Potato Soup (page 23)

Brie and Cucumber on Rye (page 77)

Brownies

Milk

HOLIDAY SKATING PARTY

Chips and dip

Lima Beans and Pork Hocks Soup (page 29)

Hot Club Sandwiches (page 81)

Apple brown betty

Hot spiced cider

(cont.)

Menus (cont.)

TEX-MEX FEAST

Nachos

Guacamole Soup (page 25)

Chicken Tacos (page 85)

Citrus fruit salad

Cinnamon cookies

Beer

SEAFOOD EXTRAVAGANZA

Shrimp cocktail

New England Clam Chowder (page 43)

Broiled Seafood Sandwiches (page 89)

Turtle sundaes

Lemonade

CHILDREN'S SLUMBER PARTY

Flavored popcorn

Beans and Franks Soup (page 32)

Peanut Butter BLT Sandwiches (page 77)

Mixed cookies

Chocolate milk

INDEX

Vice-President and Publisher: Anne M. Zeman
Senior Editor: Rebecca W. Atwater
Editor: Anne Ficklen
Assistant Editor: Rachel Simon
Photographer: Anthony Johnson
Food Stylist: Paul Grimes
Prop Stylist: Sharland Blanchard
Art Directors: Patricia Fabricant, Frederick J. Latasa
Production Manager: Lessley Davis
Assistant Managing Editor: Kimberly A. Ebert

112